TRUE OR FALSE?

- [ ] I have very few faults
- [ ] I am success-oriented
- [ ] Love is important in my life
- [ ] I have difficulty making commitments
- [ ] I usually do not like authority
- [ ] I believe life is often a "vale of tears"
- [ ] Sometimes I let people take
      advantage of me
- [ ] I look forward to new challenges
- [ ] I know that I can endure whatever
      problems arise in my life

FIND OUT WHAT YOUR ANSWERS TO THESE AND OTHER QUESTIONS REVEAL ABOUT YOU

THE ENNEAGRAM PERSONALITY TEST

YOUR SECRET SELF

ALAN FENSIN and GEORGE RYAN

AVON BOOKS ◆ NEW YORK

YOUR SECRET SELF is an original publication of Avon Books. This work has never before appeared in book form.

AVON BOOKS
A division of
The Hearst Corporation
1350 Avenue of the Americas
New York, New York 10019

First Avon Books Printing: January 1993

AVON TRADEMARK REG. U.S. PAT. OFF. AND IN OTHER COUNTRIES, MARCA REGISTRADA, HECHO EN U.S.A.

Printed in the U.S.A.

RA 10 9 8 7 6 5 4 3 2 1

Acknowledgments

I would like to thank two of my enneagram teachers, Ed Hackerson and Thomas Mellin, for their assistance. I also want to thank Martha Balser, Joanne Cohen, Severine Singh, Adel Hackerson, Cathy McCully, Cris Westfeldt, Elizabeth Fensin, and Leslie Fensin for help in putting this book together.

A.F.

Contents

YOUR
SECRET
SELF

Part One

The Enneagram and Quick Test

1

The Enneagram

The enneagram is a nine-pointed star in a circle, and it is part of an ancient method of looking deep into the human personality. Only in the twentieth century has the enneagram become familiar to many in the Western world. With workshops generating interest across the United States and Europe, its reputation is spreading quickly.

This book shows you how to use the enneagram to examine your own personality and that of loved ones, friends, and even adversaries. Using the enneagram, you can probe into the hidden motivations behind your behavior and reveal the deep-seated emotions that are so central to your life—and the lives of others.

This opening chapter explains what the enneagram is and how it developed. In the next chapter, the Quick Test tells you which enneagram personality type you are. Part Two consists of the True or False Test, which enables you to define more closely your personality type. Most people also use the True or False Test to double-check or reinforce the result of the Quick Test.

After you have found your enneagram personality type, you will also discover more detailed descriptions of your type and other personalities in Part Three: The Personality Types. The final section of the book is titled Further into the Enneagram.

Additional score sheets at the end of the book permit others to take the Quick Test and True or False Test, so that you or they can find their personality types.

The Enneagram Symbol

Is the enneagram a magic symbol of some kind? The answer is no. It has no power in itself.

The star-shaped lines in a circle represent the nine personality types of a system that has come down to us over two thousand years or more. The diagram is an ancient geometer's way of illustrating these nine main personality types and the relationships among them (see opposite). The personality types are located on equidistant points on the circle, and the lines connecting the points indicate the relationships.

The enneagram was not found carved in stone on a tomb in the desert by an archaeologist. It is not an indecipherable hieroglyph or a relic from a vanished civilization. It was passed from generation to generation over the centuries in an oral tradition that was at times secret. For something to be passed down in this way, it must have a continuous use or fill some continuing need. We do know that the enneagram has always been used to delve into the mysteries of human personality.

Since the enneagram has been around so long, isn't it out of date by now? Not any more than the human personality is. Over the ages, we humans have transformed the world around us but have remained psychologically unchanged. We are physically bigger and healthier, and we live several times as long as we once did, but we are no smarter and no more complex than we were more than three thousand years ago. So far as our personalities are concerned, we have not changed at all over that long period. We know this from the writings of the ancient Greeks and Chinese. If Ulysses or an emperor of ancient China time-traveled to America today, he would no doubt be amazed by our

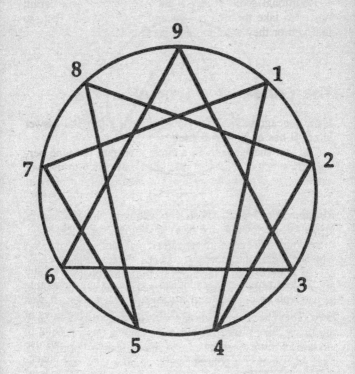

technology and perhaps by our life-styles—but not at all by our personalities. Same old thing. He'd have met people like us before.

The Three Emotional Groups

The enneagram probably originated with the discovery that all humans can be divided according to their emotions into three groups: a relationship group, an anger group, and a fear group. These groups can be represented by a triangle within a circle (see next page).

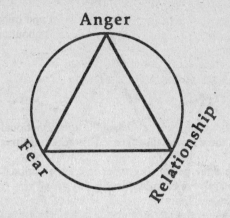

Relationship Group. Those who belong to the relationship group (also known as the heart group) are perceived to be more emotional and more concerned with feelings than those who belong to the other two groups. Note we said "perceived to be." Under the surface, those who belong to the other two groups are just as emotional. However, members of the relationship group display their emotions more publicly. They are also concerned with the way they look and the image they project. They dress in a variety of ways—anything from executive suits to ripped jeans—but they all have in common a consciousness of how they and others look.

Anger Group. The anger group is also known as the gut group, since people who belong to it tend to act from gut feelings. They are more spontaneous in their instinctive or intuitive reactions than the more calculating members of the fear group. Anger is a frequent issue in their relationships. Their anger may be either cold or hot, or their behavior may even indicate a denial of anger.

Fear Group. Those who belong to the fear group are most comfortable as rational thinkers and are therefore often called the head group. Since coping with the world is a major concern, they use logic to try to make sense of reality. They are seen by some as objective and impersonal people. Ironically, much of their thinking is about personal relationships.

Emotional Groups and Personality Types

In the enneagram system, each of the three emotional groups contains three personality types. This relationship is shown below.

Of the three personality types in each emotional group, one is central. For example, personality type Three is central in the relationship group. Of the two remaining personality types, one is regarded as being oriented toward the world (in this case Two), and the other away from the world (in this case Four). Here you could say that Twos would tend to be extroverts, and Fours introverts.

The chart on the next page shows these relationships between the three emotional groups and the nine enneagram personality types.

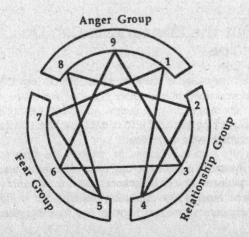

Group	Personality Type	Characteristic
Relationship	Two (extroverts)	Overrelates to people
	Three	Denies own feelings, assumes image and role from society
	Four (introverts)	Relates to self-image
Anger	Eight (extroverts)	Expresses hot anger to others
	Nine	Denies own anger, avoids conflict
	One (introverts)	Keeps cold anger within
Fear	Seven (extroverts)	Escapes fear through plans and diversions
	Six	Alternates between avoiding and confronting fear
	Five (introverts)	Escapes fear by withdrawing and not being involved.

What the Enneagram Can Do for You

Your personality is the total effect of your emotional and behavioral tendencies—what you feel and how you act. Your character traits, attitudes, and habits distinguish you from other people and yet, at the same time, identify you as a certain type of person.

In any kind of relationship, there is one chance in nine that the other person has the same enneagram personality type as yourself. The differences between two people of the same personality type can usually be attributed to differences in their life experiences. Things that have happened to us previously tend to shape our perception of what is presently taking place. Thus, two people of the same personality type who have had generally similar experiences in their lives can be expected to closely resemble each other. (This does not mean that they will like each other!) On the other hand, very different life experiences can cause two people of the same personality type to wonder what they have in common. However, although they superficially do not resemble one another, once they get to know one another better they often discover that their basic outlook and emotional orientation are the same.

In eight out of nine encounters with people, you will meet a personality type different from your own. Most people prefer the novelty of dealing with people unlike themselves, especially when things are going well. It is only when difficulties or misunderstandings occur that many of us really wonder for the first time what makes the other person tick. We bring much difficulty and even suffering upon ourselves because we do not think about the viewpoints of other people—even very close to us—until they oppose our own. Then we are puzzled. And outraged. What does she want from me? Why now? Knowing people's enneagram personality types can help you avoid such conflicts and misunderstandings. When you are aware of the real source of emotion behind the difficulty, you can deal directly with it, instead of endlessly arguing over trivia.

So, the most obvious use to which you can put the enneagram is to identify people, including yourself, by nine basic personality types according to predominant emotions. Once you recognize the predominant emotion behind another person's actions, you might be able to respond to that person in a more effective way.

On another level, you can use the enneagram to learn more about yourself and, as a result, lead a more rewarding life. Here are some of the ways in which the enneagram can play a major role in helping you achieve this goal.

• People relate better to others when they become aware of the feelings that trigger their own behavior.

- People cope better with stress when they can identify their emotional strengths and vulnerabilities.

- People are more confident when they know more about themselves and others.

History of the Enneagram

No one is sure exactly when or where the enneagram originated. It may have been in Babylon about twenty-five hundred years ago, or elsewhere in the Middle East or Afghanistan. Some claim that it was known to the ancient Zoroastrians, and perhaps also to Pythagoras, of geometry fame. *Ennea* is the Greek word for "nine," and *grammos* is the word for "points."

About nine hundred years ago, an Islamic mystical sect called the Sufis may have incorporated the enneagram into their culture, which was highly advanced. Presumably the Sufis and other groups refined it and adapted it in other ways to suit the way they lived. Or perhaps it has been passed down through the ages in almost unaltered form. We will never know. This lack of historical perspective—typical for things passed on in the oral tradition—irks some and intrigues others.

Uncertainty and mystery also surround the widespread introduction of the enneagram into modern society. The mystic George Ivanovitch Gurdjieff spread word about it from Paris in the 1920s. However, Gurdjieff himself was a bit of a mystery, even to those who knew him well. He had a wide acquaintance with Eastern religions and mystic traditions, so it seems possible that he came across the enneagram in these studies.

Many of the concepts relating to the nine enneagram personality types came from Oscar Ichazo, the founder of the Arica Institute. He said they were taught to him by Sufis in the Pamir in Afghanistan before he ever read Gurdjieff. And another man, a psychiatrist named Claudio Naranjo, correlated much ancient enneagram knowledge with modern psychiatric discoveries.

Many people have speculated, and others have followed evidence to fascinating conclusions—but researching the past is not the purpose of this book. We have only one goal, and that is to help you find your own enneagram personality type and develop the skill to tell that of others.

2

The Quick Test

Finding your enneagram personality type through the Quick Test is taking a shortcut. You will find what you need to know with the least effort and in the least amount of time, but you will know only things relevant to yourself. For this reason, it is important that you also take the True or False Test. This should be the step after you have satisfied your curiosity with the Quick Test and looked up your personality characteristics in Chapter 3.

To take the Quick Test, read the following twenty-seven statements and determine your level of agreement with each statement. You should record your reactions quickly and without prolonged examination. The score sheet is at the end of the statements (on pages 14–15), and you will find additional score sheets at the back of the book. The number 10 represents your greatest agreement with the statement, and 1 represents your least agreement.

1. I impress others as being a perfectionist.
2. I have a cold anger rather than the kind that boils over.
3. I like others to see me as highly principled.
4. I listen to others with concern and empathy.
5. I have few personal needs.
6. I like being needed, and being able to help others.

12

7. People consider me to be competitive and successful.
8. I try to be efficient in my business and personal life.
9. Failure and disgrace are about the worst things that could happen to me.

10. I could not live an average or commonplace life.
11. I see myself as a unique and creative person.
12. People see me as an emotional, feeling person.

13. I prefer to gather all available information and then decide issues logically.
14. I am a knowledgeable person.
15. I could not live a barren or meaningless life.

16. I consider myself loyal.
17. I am alert to the dangers around me.
18. I follow the rules.

19. Pain and suffering are about the worst things that could happen to me.
20. I am optimistic, and problems usually don't get me down.
21. I am talented in a variety of areas.

22. People often think of me as a leader.
23. I am a self-confident and powerful person.
24. I cannot respect people who are weak.

25. I impress others as being a peaceful person.
26. I am easy-going and comfortable.
27. I could not live with a lot of disharmony or conflict in my life.

Quick Test Score Sheet

1. 1   2   3   4   5   6   7   8   9   10
   least agreement   most agreement
2. 1   2   3   4   5   6   7   8   9   10
   least agreement   most agreement
3. 1   2   3   4   5   6   7   8   9   10
   least agreement   most agreement

4. 1   2   3   4   5   6   7   8   9   10
   least agreement   most agreement
5. 1   2   3   4   5   6   7   8   9   10
   least agreement   most agreement
6. 1   2   3   4   5   6   7   8   9   10
   least agreement   most agreement

7. 1   2   3   4   5   6   7   8   9   10
   least agreement   most agreement
8. 1   2   3   4   5   6   7   8   9   10
   least agreement   most agreement
9. 1   2   3   4   5   6   7   8   9   10
   least agreement   most agreement

10. 1   2   3   4   5   6   7   8   9   10
    least agreement   most agreement
11. 1   2   3   4   5   6   7   8   9   10
    least agreement   most agreement
12. 1   2   3   4   5   6   7   8   9   10
    least agreement   most agreement

13. 1   2   3   4   5   6   7   8   9   10
    least agreement   most agreement
14. 1   2   3   4   5   6   7   8   9   10
    least agreement   most agreement
15. 1   2   3   4   5   6   7   8   9   10
    least agreement   most agreement

16. 1   2   3   4   5   6   7   8   9   10
    least agreement   most agreement
17. 1   2   3   4   5   6   7   8   9   10
    least agreement   most agreement
18. 1   2   3   4   5   6   7   8   9   10
    least agreement   most agreement

Quick Test Score Sheet (cont.)

19. 1	2	3	4	5	6	7	8	9	10
least agreement							most agreement		
20. 1	2	3	4	5	6	7	8	9	10
least agreement							most agreement		
21. 1	2	3	4	5	6	7	8	9	10
least agreement							most agreement		
22. 1	2	3	4	5	6	7	8	9	10
least agreement							most agreement		
23. 1	2	3	4	5	6	7	8	9	10
least agreement							most agreement		
24. 1	2	3	4	5	6	7	8	9	10
least agreement							most agreement		
25. 1	2	3	4	5	6	7	8	9	10
least agreement							most agreement		
26. 1	2	3	4	5	6	7	8	9	10
least agreement							most agreement		
27. 1	2	3	4	5	6	7	8	9	10
least agreement							most agreement		

Transfer your scores from the score sheet to the following boxes. Total the scores in each of the nine boxes. (There are additional sets of boxes at the back of the book.)

Quick Test Boxes

1._____	4._____	7._____
2._____	5._____	8._____
3._____	6._____	9._____
Total _____	Total _____	Total _____
Personality	Personality	Personality
Type One	Type Two	Type Three

10._____	13._____	16._____
11._____	14._____	17._____
12._____	15._____	18._____
Total _____	Total _____	Total _____
Personality	Personality	Personality
Type Four	Type Five	Type Six

19._____	22._____	25._____
20._____	23._____	26._____
21._____	24._____	27._____
Total _____	Total _____	Total _____
Personality	Personality	Personality
Type Seven	Type Eight	Type Nine

As labeled, each box represents a personality type, numbered One through Nine. Circle the four boxes with the highest scores. (Circle five boxes if there is a tie score.)

For each of the four or five boxes you circle, read the characteristics for those personality types in Chapter 3. If one description fits you well, this is almost certainly your true personality type. Some people discover their personality type at this stage, but a more definitive conclusion can be reached after taking the True or False Test.

If two or more of the descriptions seem to fit you, don't let that stop you. This happens to most people. It's not an indication of strength or weakness or complexity of your personality. All it means is that your personality type did not respond to the Quick Test and that you need to take the longer True or False Test.

3

Characteristics of Personality Types

The characteristics given in this chapter for each personality type are merely thumbnail sketches to aid you in finding your type. More detailed information on each personality type is given later. In the enneagram system, people are referred to according to personality type, such as Ones or Fours. This does sound a bit impersonal. To avoid this, some writers have given names to each type. In discussing Threes, for example, one writer has given the name Status Seeker and another the name Performer. Of course, Threes can be both status seekers and performers, but neither of these names describes the personality type completely—and thus both can be misleading. For want of a more satisfactory system, we will stick with numbers.

Ones

Ones usually try to do their best, and are sometimes called perfectionists. They mean well but find fault in themselves and in others. They frequently have very high standards and principles. Ones seldom feel that things are good enough as they are, and so are likely to try harder than others. They are in control most of the time but occasionally can find themselves out of balance. Ones are capable of powerful jealousy and rage but rarely express these emotions.

Twos

Personal relationships are extremely important to Twos. Normally they are caring, empathetic, sensitive, and believe in helping or saving others. Twos are generous, and people often ask their advice or seek their comfort. However, they are sometimes oversolicitous and smother others with love. When Twos give, they need something back, such as appreciation. They can go back and forth between, on one hand, needing people and wanting people to need them and, on the other hand, not needing people and not wanting people to need them. Twos usually have intense feelings and laugh or cry easily. They are very concerned with what others think of them.

Threes

Typically Threes are competitive, fit in well with their peer group, and are concerned with how they appear to others. They are mostly self-assured, cheerful, and rarely depressed. However, Threes tend not to show their real feelings. Usually good students, they put much effort into being successful and are practical and efficient in planning and in accomplishing goals. They love to work and keep active; sometimes they don't know how to stop working. Threes are usually good talkers, but can be difficult to connect with on a personal level.

Fours

Fours are often introspective, esthetic, moody, and feel themselves to be different from others. They like to analyze their feelings and motivations, and those of others. Although they can be artistic and sensitive, they sometimes feel lost and depressed. Fours are often creative, spontaneous people who do things with a flair. They can feel superior to people they perceive as less original. They appreciate the beauty of nature and are often flamboyant dressers.

Fives

Fives can be somewhat introverted and have few close friends. Usually they keep their feelings to themselves, and they can be eccentric. Although they tend to have a soft, sweet quality, in truth they are difficult to get to know. Analytical and theoretical, they tend to be stingy with both knowledge and money. Self-sufficient, they can easily spend time alone. Fives usually want to understand why things work the way they do, and can become experts in their field. They have a hard time confronting others, and tend to have a sense of irony and the absurd.

Sixes

Sixes believe in rules and duty. They are usually loyal and committed to family, friends, and employer. Sixes believe life can be very demanding, and are very sensitive to dangers in their environment. They can put great effort into structuring their life in order to avoid danger. Sixes tend to intellectualize and like to play with words. They want to be sure of all the facts before making a decision.

Sevens

Sevens talk about ideas rather than share feelings. They are more likely to plan or fantasize than to take action. Usually fun people, they are more into joy and celebration than into suffering or gloom. Sevens often look for the sweetness and happiness in life, but are prone to get bored with routines. Sometimes they have several plans or projects going simultaneously. Their plans revolve around how to avoid dealing with their fears.

Eights

Generally strong, self-confident people, Eights are capable of confronting others but also have a sweet side. They are practical and resourceful. Eights often like to be center stage. Usually matter-of-fact, open, and honest, they tend to dislike intellectuals. They work hard and campaign to right wrongs, are aware of where power lies, and really want to win. Eights tend to be proud, self-sufficient accomplishers who are often uncomfortable with emotional displays.

Nines

Easy-going, stable people, Nines can usually see both sides of a situation. They prefer to avoid conflict, and others feel comfortable to be around them. Normally they have varied interests and are cheerful, peaceful, and balanced. They may watch a lot of television and fall asleep easily. There is a sense of immobility about them. Nines can be stubborn, and once they are set they are difficult to change.

Part Two

The True or False Test

4

Taking the True
or False Test

You may find it difficult to decide which personality type
best fits you, or you may have decided on your personality
type and are just double-checking. In either case, you take
this test in the same manner as The Quick Test. You should
answer all your questions for one type choice all the way
through before working on the next type possibility.

Taking this test is easy. There are fifty True or False
statements and fifty answers for each personality type. The
statements are on the right-hand pages, and the answers are
on the left-hand pages. The True or False Score Sheet is at
the end of this test, on page 127. (There are additional True
or False Score Sheets at the end of the book.)

Here is how you begin. Select your potential personality
type and read the appropriate statement in #1 True or False.
How does the statement apply to you? Then turn to the next
page and look at #1 Answers.

- If you agree with the answer, make a check on the score
  sheet.
- If you disagree with the answer, make a zero on the
  score sheet.
- If you can't decide on an answer, leave the space blank.

Continue until you have considered all fifty statements and answers for that personality type.

People change as they mature—so if you are in doubt about the answer to a question, answer as you would have when you were younger.

Interpretations of your results can be found following the score sheet.

#1
True
or
False?

Ones: I usually avoid getting angry.

Twos: I decide things more on gut feelings than on logic.

Threes: I usually dress well.

Fours: I think of myself as special.

Fives: I like to work most of the time.

Sixes: I believe the world to be a safe place.

Sevens: I find life full of difficulties.

Eights: I tell it like it is.

Nines: I pay attention to how I look and the clothes I wear.

#1
Answers

Ones have difficulty realizing and expressing their anger.   True.

Twos often rely on their intuition rather than logic.   True.

Threes are concerned with the appearance they make.   True.

Fours usually believe themselves to be above average.   True.

Fives enjoy their free time.   False.

Sixes find life somewhat threatening.   False.

Sevens love life and avoid negative thinking. False.

Eights tell you exactly what they think of pussyfooting around.   True.

Nines are generally unconcerned with their dress. False.

#2
True
or
False?

Ones: I am often intolerant of faults in others.

Twos: I do good works without expecting credit for them.

Threes: I am not very competitive.

Fours: I often dwell on suffering.

Fives: I like being by myself.

Sixes: I am sensitive to my surroundings.

Sevens: I know that I have many problems.

Eights: I am a loyal friend.

Nines: I am a high-energy type.

#2
Answers

Ones expect the best of themselves and others. True.

Twos often do good deeds without openly demanding credit, yet, on a less conscious level, they want recognition for their efforts.   False.

Threes are quite competitive.   False.

Fours can dwell on sadness and loss.   True.

Fives do not like to share all their time with others.   True.

Sixes often look for hidden dangers.   True.

Sevens tend to deny the existence of a problem. False.

Eights are loyal to family and friends and will fight to protect them.   True.

Nines are usually low-energy people.   False.

#3
True
or
False?

Ones: I have very few faults.

Twos: I often take care of other people.

Threes: I am good at promoting things.

Fours: I am not very emotional.

Fives: I am generally self-sufficient.

Sixes: I usually don't judge by appearances.

Sevens: I spend much time resolving problems.

Eights: I seldom use abusive language.

Nines: I thrive on conflict.

#3
Answers

Ones usually believe they are imperfect and are concerned with correcting their faults.   False.

Twos tend to look out for other people.   True.

Threes often promote themselves or their ideas.   True.

Fours can have strong and deep emotions.   False.

Fives like to rely on themselves rather than others.   True.

Sixes are good at seeing beyond the apparent.   True.

Sevens look for the sweetness in life and ignore the problems.   False.

Eights have no difficulty in becoming loud or insulting.   False.

Nines do not handle conflict very well.   False.

#4
True
or
False?

Ones: I believe there is a lot in life that needs improving.

Twos: I seldom cry.

Threes: I am success-oriented.

Fours: I have a sense of style.

Fives: I am not very good at manipulation.

Sixes: I understand underlying meanings.

Sevens: I have had many jobs.

Eights: I don't like strength in others.

Nines: I usually lead a harmonious life.

#4
Answers

Ones are keenly aware of the imperfections of life and often want to correct them.   True.

Twos are easily moved to tears.   False.

Threes, more than most people, dislike failure.   True.

Fours demonstrate flair and style.   True.

Fives can manipulate people and events, and are seldom caught doing it.   False.

Sixes can see beyond the obvious.   True.

Sevens often have had more than the normal number of jobs.   True.

Eights usually have much respect for people who stand up to them.   False.

Nines avoid disturbing situations.   True.

#5
True
or
False?

Ones: I am a meticulous worker.

Twos: Love is important in my life.

Threes: I am more concerned about who I am than how I look.

Fours: I am rarely sad.

Fives: I can easily accept management by others.

Sixes: I like words.

Sevens: I have had many important relationships.

Eights: I recognize my own weaknesses.

Nines: I am enthusiastic about life.

#5
Answers

Ones give time and attention to every detail.
True.

Twos believe loving relationships are of vital
importance.   True.

Threes are very concerned with how they appear
to others.   False.

Fours usually have sadness in their lives.   False.

Fives have a fear of being controlled.   False.

Sixes like quotes and interesting phrases.   True.

Sevens often have more than the normal number
of relationships.   True.

Eights usually deny any weakness in themselves.
False.

Nines are laid-back people and seldom get very
excited.   False.

#6
True
or
False?

Ones: When I do get angry, it is a cold contained anger.

Twos: I have more needs than the average person.

Threes: I easily get depressed.

Fours: I often wear unique clothing.

Fives: I have difficulty making commitments.

Sixes: I trust myself completely.

Sevens: I often plan for the future.

Eights: I believe the world is a hard and tough place.

Nines: I see myself as very special.

#6
Answers

Ones usually suppress their anger.   True.

Twos avoid recognizing their needs and so often believe they have none.   False.

Threes are usually cheerful.   False.

Fours often accent their clothing with an unusual scarf, hat, or bold jewelry.   True.

Fives have a fear of committing themselves.   True.

Sixes do not trust themselves and prefer definite rules.   False.

Sevens are often busy planning the next thing to do.   True.

Eights often see the world as a hostile place that needs to be conquered.   True.

Nines are unpretentious and downplay their own importance.   False.

#7
True
or
False?

Ones: I like the status quo.

Twos: I like to be needed.

Threes: I believe in dressing for success.

Fours: I am aware of my feelings.

Fives: I am not very loyal to other people.

Sixes: Things often go wrong.

Sevens: I usually do not like authority.

Eights: I am not a vengeful person.

Nines: I like to spend time watching TV or reading a book.

#7
Answers

Ones believe things are not good enough the way they are.   False.

Twos want to be needed and loved by others.   True.

Threes usually know how to dress well.   True.

Fours like to analyze their emotions.   True.

Fives are very loyal, once they have made a commitment.   False.

Sixes often imagine things going awry.   True.

Sevens often have a difficult time dealing with authority.   True.

Eights, when wronged, often think of revenge.   False.

Nines enjoy sitting back in a comfortable chair and taking it easy.   True.

#8
True
or
False?

Ones: I like to be in control of the world around me.

Twos: I notice that very few people depend on me for help.

Threes: I can be compulsive about my work.

Fours: I believe life is often a "vale of tears."

Fives: I can be very stubborn.

Sixes: I strongly fear making the wrong decision.

Sevens: I often judge other people.

Eights: I can identify with patriotic heroes.

Nines: I like lots of excitement in my life.

#8
Answers

Ones like to feel in control of their environment.
  True.

Twos have many people who depend on them.
  False.

Threes are often obsessive about their jobs.
  True.

Fours often focus on unobtainable or lost loves.
  True.

Fives can be stubborn once they make a
  decision.   True.

Sixes fear blame if they are wrong.   True.

Sevens are usually nonjudgmental.   False.

Eights like patriotic heroes who embody strength,
  power, and success.   True.

Nines like the repetition of familiar events.
  False.

#9
True
or
False?

Ones: I get uncomfortable when others compliment me.

Twos: I like to serve others.

Threes: I usually have a winning smile.

Fours: I experience much love in my life.

Fives: I don't like being emotional.

Sixes: I don't like rules and laws.

Sevens: I don't mind following other people.

Eights: Sometimes I let people take advantage of me.

Nines: I sometimes have difficulty meeting deadlines.

#9
Answers

Ones do not believe they deserve compliments.
   True.

Twos strive to advise and care for their friends.
   True.

Threes can put on a good face to impress others.
   True.

Fours seldom seem to have enough love.
   False.

Fives prefer to remain the observer.   True.

Sixes usually obey the letter of the law.   False.

Sevens do not like to be told what to do.
   False.

Eights do not let anyone take advantage of
   them.   False.

Nines seem to have difficulty in getting really
   motivated.   True.

#10
True
or
False?

Ones: My life runs smoothly when I follow rules.

Twos: I seldom compliment others.

Threes: I am not status-conscious.

Fours: I have a lot of drama in my life.

Fives: I don't share all my knowledge with others.

Sixes: I am seldom apprehensive.

Sevens: I dream of having many children.

Eights: I am sometimes seen as rebellious.

Nines: I shift gears slowly when moving from task to task.

#10
Answers

Ones are most happy when they are doing things according to the rules.   True.

Twos often compliment their friends.   False.

Threes are very concerned with how they compare to others.   False.

Fours often have dramatic events happening around them.   True.

Fives are somewhat secretive with their knowledge.   True.

Sixes often experience anxiety and fear.   False.

Sevens usually avoid circumstances that tie them down.   False.

Eights are sometimes seen by others as defying authority, since they want to establish their own authority.   True.

Nines change direction only very slowly, and once they do they tend to remain pointed toward the new destination.   True.

#11
True
or
False?

Ones: I have a lot of "shoulds" and "oughts" in my life.

Twos: I can manipulate others fairly well.

Threes: I try to be competent and precise.

Fours: I desire to be connected with others.

Fives: I enjoy being busy.

Sixes: I look forward to new challenges.

Sevens: I am not good at showing my feelings.

Eights: I have been called an intellectual.

Nines: I am a solid, substantial person.

#11
Answers

Ones know the rules and usually follow them.
True.

Twos are great manipulators.   True.

Threes are interested in getting good results.
True.

Fours would like to be merged with their
partners.   True.

Fives usually are upset if they have too much to
do.   False.

Sixes often prefer repeating their past successful
experiences.   False.

Sevens resist exhibiting anxiety or other disturbing
feelings.   True.

Eights dislike intellectuals and see them as playing
games.   False.

Nines are usually very stable.   True.

#12
True
or
False?

Ones: I resent authority.

Twos: I seldom feel that my friends use me.

Threes: I am not an aggressive person.

Fours: I am seldom ashamed of anything.

Fives: I sometimes act before getting all the facts.

Sixes: I am an independent person.

Sevens: I consider myself a rebel.

Eights: I almost always stand up for myself.

Nines: I have a calming effect on those around me.

#12
Answers

Ones can accept rules and authority if they do not compromise their integrity.   False.

Twos sometimes feel used.   False.

Threes can be fairly aggressive in getting things done.   False.

Fours can feel much shame.   False.

Fives usually gather knowledge and fear direct action.   False.

Sixes usually do not seek independence.   False.

Sevens are often nonconformists.   True.

Eights usually speak out for themselves, even if it means confrontation.   True.

Nines, with their soothing, gentle way, often help others relax.   True.

#13
True
or
False?

Ones: I am not very emotional.

Twos: I require little attention or appreciation from others.

Threes: I can't trust others to do as good a job as myself.

Fours: I am not overly concerned when my friends get sick.

Fives: I dislike others watching me.

Sixes: I am a warm and hospitable person.

Sevens: I am a good storyteller.

Eights: I often inspire courage and strength in others.

Nines: I sometimes have difficulty in getting to sleep.

#13
Answers

Ones often repress their emotions.   True.

Twos want their friends to care for them, be close
   to them, and appreciate their help.   False.

Threes can be good at delegating work to others
   but often believe they are the only ones who
   can do it right.   True.

Fours can get quite upset when their loved ones
   or friends are sick.   False.

Fives like to observe but dislike being observed.
   True.

Sixes usually make warm and faithful friends.
   True.

Sevens tell good stories.   True.

Eights often give inspiration and courage to
   others.   True.

Nines tend to sleep very well.   False.

#14
True
or
False?

Ones: I dress appropriately.

Twos: I seldom flatter others.

Threes: I make things work out to my benefit.

Fours: I don't like people to expect things of me.

Fives: I usually solve problems by thinking about them.

Sixes: I seldom have doubts.

Sevens: I sometimes play the clown.

Eights: I am not very assertive.

Nines: I have only so much energy, so I try to conserve it.

#14
Answers

Ones often have a sense of what is proper in their dress.   True.

Twos often flatter their friends to make them feel good.   False.

Threes believe they can make life work.   True.

Fours resist doing things that are expected of them.   True.

Fives place their emphasis on logic.   True.

Sixes can feel quite insecure.   False.

Sevens like to joke and are fun to be around.   True.

Eights can be aggressive when speaking out for what they think is right.   False.

Nines tend to tire easily.   True.

#15
True
or
False?

Ones: I take care of my business dealings.

Twos: I display emotion easily.

Threes: I dislike incompetence in others.

Fours: I don't like to break rules.

Fives: I love to be in competition with others.

Sixes: I have few duties or obligations.

Sevens: I usually don't rationalize.

Eights: I seldom get bored.

Nines: I let things bother me.

#15
Answers

Ones try to do the best they can.   True.

Twos readily act on their feelings.   True.

Threes have little patience with ineffectiveness in others.   True.

Fours enjoy breaking rules—so long as they don't get caught.   False.

Fives avoid competing with others.   False.

Sixes usualy feel they have many responsibilities. False.

Sevens sometimes rationalize as a defense mechanism.   False.

Eights like new experiences and can get bored easily.   False.

Nines avoid facing facts that can cause them anxiety.   False.

#16
True
or
False?

Ones: I believe this would be a better world if people had better manners.

Twos: I am known as a very sweet person.

Threes: I was a good student.

Fours: I sometimes feel depressed.

Fives: I often have trouble getting started.

Sixes: I seldom take sides in an argument.

Sevens: I don't have much formal education.

Eights: I am a hard worker.

Nines: I actively care about my loved ones' well-being.

#16
Answers

Ones would prefer for everyone to behave properly.   True.

Twos are sometimes sticky sweet.   True.

Threes often were well-behaved children.   True.

Fours can experience serious depression.   True.

Fives have difficulty getting started, but once started they can be very focused on what they are doing.   True.

Sixes often choose the side they believe right.   False.

Sevens are often well educated.   False.

Eights have a work ethic and can be very demanding of themselves.   True.

Nines can be supportive and generous with family and friends.   True.

#17
True
or
False?

Ones: I could write a "Miss Manners" column in a newspaper.

Twos: I am competitive and unwilling to let others win.

Threes: I tend to watch from the sidelines rather than play the game.

Fours: I like science and math.

Fives: I like to exhibit my many talents.

Sixes: I am often a courageous hero in my daydreams.

Sevens: I know a little about most things.

Eights: I don't mind being in the spotlight.

Nines: I do well with five hours' sleep.

#17
Answers

Ones know what is proper behavior and can act as censors of others.   True.

Twos are usually willing to let their friends win to make them feel good.   False.

Threes generally get involved in the game. False.

Fours often prefer poetry and other arts to math and science.   False.

Fives are stingy about sharing their knowledge or accomplishments.   False.

Sixes usually see themselves as champions of their cause.   True.

Sevens often have a broad, general knowledge. True.

Eights can be the center of attention if the cause is important to them.   True.

Nines usually sleep more than the average person.   False.

#18
True
or
False?

Ones: I know I am bad.

Twos: I am willing to be the power behind the throne.

Threes: I usually do things well.

Fours: I give importance to beauty.

Fives: I have many close friends.

Sixes: I like to know the meaning behind events.

Sevens: I rarely need help from other people.

Eights: I am sometimes sly or sneaky.

Nines: I believe that all problems can be solved by people working together and talking through their differences.

#18
Answers

Ones believe themselves to be good people and examples to others.   False.

Twos can be supportive and let others take the limelight.   True.

Threes are more likely to remember their successes.   True.

Fours often beautify their surroundings.   True.

Fives usually allow few people to be close to them.   False.

Sixes want to make sense out of their lives.   True.

Sevens can usually figure out most things themselves.   True.

Eights are usually matter-of-fact and open in what they do.   False.

Nines feel that tranquillity and harmony are both important and attainable.   True.

#19
True
or
False?

Ones: I tend to see things as black or white.

Twos: I sometimes fuss over others.

Threes: I like to run my own show.

Fours: I am almost never hardheaded.

Fives: I like to understand the way things work.

Sixes: I am seldom judgmental.

Sevens: I like to try new things.

Eights: I rarely tell a lie.

Nines: I know that I can endure whatever
   problems arise in my life.

#19
Answers

Ones are inclined to see things as either right or wrong.   True.

Twos usually take care of others.   True.

Threes tend to be salesmen, doctors, business owners, or follow other professions where they can run their own show.   True.

Fours can sometimes be bullheaded.   False.

Fives want to make sense of the world.   True.

Sixes can be critical when things go wrong. False.

Sevens like to taste and experience life.   True.

Eights are usually honest.   True.

Nines can endure great difficulties, although this sometimes means tuning out the problems. True.

#20
True
or
False?

Ones: I have very high standards.

Twos: I seldom talk about my personal concerns.

Threes: I have been accused of manipulating others.

Fours: I can be jealous.

Fives: I would rather be with a group than with one other person.

Sixes: I like spontaneous happenings.

Sevens: I like to work toward one goal at a time.

Eights: I know how to use power for the benefit of all.

Nines: I am open and truthful if the matter is important.

#20
Answers

Ones often have high standards of perfection that are rarely met.   True.

Twos often tell their friends about their problems. False.

Threes sometimes use others to help them get their way.   True.

Fours can be jealous and clinging, especially when in love.   True.

Fives prefer to be with one person at a time. False.

Sixes usually prefer scheduled events.   False.

Sevens like to keep all their options open all the time.   False.

Eights usually know how to acquire power and how to use it.   True.

Nines usually are diplomatic but can be very honest, and although they do not want to hurt anyone, others can be offended by this honesty.   True.

#21
True
or
False?

Ones: I pay attention to proper grooming and neat dressing.

Twos: I have many friends.

Threes: I am a good team player.

Fours: I can be a hater.

Fives: I am a storehouse of information.

Sixes: I often rationalize.

Sevens: I am concerned about good health.

Eights: I believe that revenge is wrong because it only leads to more revenge.

Nines: I don't like to upset things.

#21
Answers

Ones dress neatly and groom properly, but usually not quite up to their own standards of perfection.   True.

Twos have many people in their debt.   True.

Threes work well with others as long as the team is moving toward a goal.   True.

Fours can lash out at others when things go poorly.   True.

Fives know many facts but do not like to part with their knowledge.   True.

Sixes find excuses so as not to accept blame. True.

Sevens often think about their health and well-being.   True.

Eights, when wronged, think of revenge and can desire to punish others.   False.

Nines do not like chaos.   True.

#22
True
or
False?

Ones: I get frustrated if things don't go well.

Twos: I am often not appreciated by my friends.

Threes: I am not good at talking to other people.

Fours: I am not very spontaneous.

Fives: I find life to be full of hidden meanings.

Sixes: I have a strong sense of duty.

Sevens: I have knowledge of many different things.

Eights: I don't like to make other people upset.

Nines: I don't seek vengeance.

#22
Answers

Ones can become overly upset when things go wrong.   True.

Twos often feel unappreciated for the help they have given others.   True.

Threes are usually good at communication. False.

Fours can act with childlike spontaneity.   False.

Fives usually find life full of meanings.   True.

Sixes often do what they feel is their duty. True.

Sevens can talk at length about many subjects. True.

Eights generally are not afraid to agitate others when they believe themselves to be right. False.

Nines are peacemakers and don't seek retribution. True.

#23
True
or
False?

Ones: I am sometimes not in touch with my feelings.

Twos: I enjoy seeing others in embarrassing situations.

Threes: I like having specific and attainable goals.

Fours: I am a caring person.

Fives: My knowledge is very limited.

Sixes: I sense the contradictions in life.

Sevens: I had a happy childhood.

Eights: I don't like arrogant people.

Nines: I sometimes enjoy a good fight—if there is no other way out.

#23
Answers

Ones are often cut off from their own feelings.
  True.

Twos do not like seeing others in difficult
  situations and often pull for the underdog.
  False.

Threes usually want to see progress in achieving
  their goals.   True.

Fours are often concerned and caring about their
  friends.   True.

Fives love acquiring knowledge and know many
  facts.   False.

Sixes are usually aware of life's ambiguity.
  True.

Sevens usually remember their childhood as
  happy, but it really may have been frustrating.
  True.

Eights often have a compulsion to dethrone
  arrogant types.   True.

Nines usually will keep peace at any price.
  False.

#24
True
or
False?

Ones: I do not like hard and demanding work.

Twos: I have acted as a matchmaker.

Threes: I have difficulty in making decisions.

Fours: I like simplicity.

Fives: I often share my feelings with others.

Sixes: I sometimes think I will accomplish many good things.

Sevens: I am better at planning than at doing.

Eights: I sometimes push myself to the limit, both physically and mentally.

Nines: I get along well with people.

#24
Answers

Ones are usually hard workers and often show ambition.   False.

Twos enjoy bringing people together.   True.

Threes easily make decisions.   False.

Fours would rather not get into complicated situations.   True.

Fives tend to be very private people.   False.

Sixes sometimes imagine the many things they will do, but these usually remain just thoughts.   True.

Sevens are good planners but often have difficulty in completing their projects.   True.

Eights like a good challenge that will take them to their limits.   True.

Nines feel that harmonious relations with others are important.   True.

#25
True
or
False?

Ones: I often experience self-satisfaction.

Twos: I do not like to get close to people.

Threes: I am happiest when I am doing something.

Fours: I do not dwell on my feelings.

Fives: I can easily assert myself.

Sixes: I have strong gut reactions and feelings.

Sevens: The stories I like often have a sad ending.

Eights: I often compromise in order to solve problems.

Nines: I am interested in many different things.

#25
Answers

Ones are seldom totally satisfied with themselves.
  False.

Twos like being involved with their friends.
  False.

Threes like to be busy and are apt to be called
  people on the go.   True.

Fours have deep feelings that they dwell on for
  long periods.   False.

Fives find it difficult to be assertive.   False.

Sixes are more analytical and less intuitive.
  False.

Sevens prefer stories with happy endings.
  False.

Eights seldom compromise and instead fight for
  their beliefs.   False.

Nines have many interests, including science, art,
  and travel.   True.

#26
True
or
False?

Ones: I am a perfectionist.

Twos: I am capable of physically abusing others.

Threes: I can usually confront people with little effort.

Fours: I am often hurt by others.

Fives: I can easily ask for help from others.

Sixes: I take little on faith.

Sevens: I have more enemies than most people.

Eights: I often fight for the rights of my friends.

Nines: I am often unhappy with the way things are.

#26
Answers

Ones strive for perfection in both themselves and others.   True.

Twos are usually nonviolent.   False.

Threes usually prefer to avoid conflict.   False.

Fours are familiar with pain and separation.
True.

Fives can find it difficult to reach out to others.
False.

Sixes usually require logical proof of things.
True.

Sevens are usually liked by most people.   False.

Eights often help friends who have been wronged.   True.

Nines are generally cheerful and happy.   False

#27
True
or
False?

Ones: I often feel anxious.

Twos: I seek the warmth of friendship when things go wrong for me.

Threes: I often work on improving myself.

Fours: I find symbols meaningful.

Fives: I am good at small talk.

Sixes: I have at times been afraid I would stutter.

Sevens: I love a good party.

Eights: I do not have much excess energy.

Nines: I usually see both sides of a conflict.

#27
Answers

Ones often experience a fear of failing.   True.

Twos in trouble often find comfort in their friends.
True.

Threes direct much energy to self-improvement.
True.

Fours often find meanings in symbolic things.
True.

Fives are not at ease in social situations.   False.

Sixes sometimes have a start/stop quality in their
voice.   True.

Sevens like to have fun and enjoy parties.
True.

Eights often work with gusto and have much
stamina.   False.

Nines usually are good arbitrators because they
see the big picture.   True.

#28
True
or
False?

Ones: I am sometimes jealous of others.

Twos: My eyes are expressive.

Threes: I am a go-getter.

Fours: I am sometimes considered distant.

Fives: I am sensitive to other people's needs.

Sixes: I am not a serious person.

Sevens: I often brighten the lives of others.

Eights: I am a down-to-earth person.

Nines: I listen more than I talk.

#28
Answers

Ones can be jealous of those they feel are more accomplished than themselves.   True.

Twos often use eye contact or touching in their communication.   True.

Threes get things accomplished.   True.

Fours believe they are extraordinary people, and so others often perceive them as aloof.   True.

Fives are aware of the needs of others but often avoid getting involved.   True.

Sixes are usually serious and joke very little. False.

Sevens are usually good-natured and lighthearted with others.   True.

Eights tend to be more active rather than indecisive and cerebral.   True.

Nines have a need to know, in conversation, how others stand.   True.

#29
True
or
False?

Ones: I am an intuitive thinker.

Twos: I am a feeling person.

Threes: I want to be professional at my job.

Fours: I would rather maintain a distance from others.

Fives: I am a more logical person than a feeling person.

Sixes: I am rarely afraid of anything.

Sevens: I am sometimes excessive.

Eights: I am often an initiator or promoter of new things.

Nines: I am seldom uptight.

#29
Answers

Ones often grasp the total situation.   True.

Twos are usually feeling people.   True.

Threes strive to become accomplished at their occupation.   True.

Fours are caring people and act from the heart.   False.

Fives are usually better at rational thought than feelings.   True.

Sixes can have much apprehension about life.   False.

Sevens sometimes overconsume food, drink, drugs, and sex.   True.

Eights often quickly recognize new possibilities and may promote them.   True.

Nines are easygoing and stable.   True.

#30
True
or
False?

Ones: I strive to be better.

Twos: I often feel inadequate.

Threes: I am a good manager of my time.

Fours: I often feel like an outsider.

Fives: I am sometimes quite critical.

Sixes: I am a logical thinker.

Sevens: I am more inhibited than most people.

Eights: I easily surrender power to others when necessary.

Nines: I usually avoid people I do not relate well to.

#30
Answers

Ones try to perfect themselves.   True.

Twos can feel incompetent and unsure of their own abilities.   True.

Threes usually use time wisely.   True.

Fours feel different and separate from others. True.

Fives can find fault in everyone and every situation.   True.

Sixes generally are logical.   True.

Sevens are often rather exuberant and uninhibited. False.

Eights can be ruthless in acquiring or retaining power.   False.

Nines would rather limit their interactions to those with whom they feel at ease.   True.

#31
True
or
False?

Ones: I try to avoid blame for things that go wrong.

Twos: I have no problem about receiving help from others.

Threes: .I know how to handle money.

Fours: I am not overly interested in learning more about myself.

Fives: I ask few questions about what I observe.

Sixes: I am decisive.

Sevens: I am more a logical than a feeling type of person.

Eights: I do not like to be in charge of a group.

Nines: I do not like people to make demands on me.

#31
Answers

Ones try to do everything right.   True.

Twos have difficulty in receiving freely from others.   False.

Threes usually are good money managers.   True.

Fours have a strong need to discover their real identity.   False.

Fives want to know why and how things happen.   False.

Sixes can hesitate and waver when making decisions.   False.

Sevens do not usually dwell on emotions.   True.

Eights usually like to command.   False.

Nines try to avoid outside demands on their time and energy.   True.

#32
True
or
False?

Ones: I am not concerned with morality.

Twos: I give a lot of myself to others.

Threes: I am usually a positive person.

Fours: I had a happy childhood.

Fives: I rarely think I have enough information to begin a project.

Sixes: I am a trusting person.

Sevens: I am more of an introvert than an extrovert.

Eights: I am most often an intuitive thinker.

Nines: I generally stand up for my beliefs and for myself.

#32
Answers

Ones usually adhere to a strict personal moral
code.   False.

Twos give a lot so that they will be loved.
True.

Threes are generally positive and enthusiastic
about life.   True.

Fours usually feel they had a sad or lonely
childhood.   False.

Fives often feel they need all the facts before they
start something.   True.

Sixes often do not have faith that life will work
out.   False.

Sevens generally like being with people, though
they sometimes need time alone.   False.

Eights often have a way of knowing that goes
beyond logic.   True.

Nines usually avoid confrontation.   False.

#33
True
or
False?

Ones: I am usually organized.

Twos: I seldom help others.

Threes: I am very competitive.

Fours: I am different from most people.

Fives: I have many friends.

Sixes: I am a reliable worker.

Sevens: I seldom talk about my feelings.

Eights: I am sometimes defenseless.

Nines: I am usually intuitive.

#33
Answers

Ones usually organize themselves to get things done more efficiently.   True.

Twos often nurture and take care of others.   False.

Threes are often serious game-players in business and elsewhere.   True.

Fours consider themselves unlike average people.   True.

Fives can have shaky relationships.   False.

Sixes usually are reliable and hardworking.   True.

Sevens prefer to talk about ideas rather than feelings.   True.

Eights are usually strong, self-confident people who command respect from others.   False.

Nines usually have good gut reactions.   True.

#34
True
or
False?

Ones: I believe that if I don't do things, no one will.

Twos: I feel it is good to be close to people.

Threes: I am efficient.

Fours: I enjoy being spontaneous.

Fives: I have an analytical mind.

Sixes: I find life quite demanding.

Sevens: I have many different interests in my life.

Eights: I am sentimental.

Nines: I worry a lot.

#34
Answers

Ones usually believe that very few people can do things as correctly as they can.   True.

Twos usually like to be close to others, and often hug them.   True.

Threes efficiently accomplish tasks.   True.

Fours prefer a spontaneous, creative life.   True.

Fives are usually logical.   True.

Sixes usually find life demanding and serious.   True.

Sevens have varied plans and projects.   True.

Eights are usually uncomfortable with sentimentality.   False.

Nines seldom worry and usually don't believe they have sizable problems.   False.

#35
True
or
False?

Ones: I usually feel very good about myself.

Twos: I'm usually unconcerned about what others think of me.

Threes: I am unimpressed by the trappings of success.

Fours: I often get into long conversations.

Fives: I can be somewhat intense.

Sixes: I am a good family member.

Sevens: I like to plan and fantasize.

Eights: I can be a formidable negotiator.

Nines: I am content with life.

#35
Answers

Ones seldom feel things are good enough.
  False.

Twos are concerned about what others think.
  False.

Threes like to appear successful and make a good
  impression.   False.

Fours often speak with others and think over their
  conversations.   True.

Fives can totally lose themselves in things.
  True.

Sixes generally believe in loyalty and duty.
  True.

Sevens are more likely to plan or fantasize than to
  take action.   True.

Eights are usually stubborn in trying to get their
  way.   True.

Nines are usually content and balanced.   True.

#36
True
or
False?

Ones: I've been told I am a perfectionist.

Twos: I often think about my friendships.

Threes: Others see me as successful.

Fours: I do things with flair.

Fives: I am generous in sharing my possessions.

Sixes: I often seek the advice of others.

Sevens: I hate being bored.

Eights: I want to make a lot of money.

Nines: I am somewhat conservative in my beliefs.

#36
Answers

Ones often try harder than others to get things right.   True.

Twos often have a number of close friends.   True.

Threes usually dress or behave so that others will see them as successful.   True.

Fours are creative and do things with a flair.   True.

Fives tend to be stingy with their things.   False.

Sixes often fear making decisions and seek the advice of others.   True.

Sevens usually do lots of things so they won't be bored.   True.

Eights often have various money-making activities.   True.

Nines often have conservative values.   True.

#37
True
or
False?

Ones: I sometimes resent others enjoying life.

Twos: I look out for myself.

Threes: I sometimes have difficulty in finishing jobs.

Fours: I am sometimes envious of others.

Fives: I dislike being alone.

Sixes: I am consistent.

Sevens: I sometimes want to be the center of attention.

Eights: I can be negative and pessimistic.

Nines: I believe it is difficult to change things.

#37
Answers

Ones can be resentful when things go poorly for them.   True.

Twos are self-sufficient.   True.

Threes usually are good at completing things. False.

Fours can experience envy when others succeed.   True.

Fives enjoy doing things on their own.   False.

Sixes usually like stability in their lives.   True.

Sevens often do things to attract attention to themselves.   True.

Eights are usually positive and optimistic. False.

Nines are fatalistic and usually do not exert the energy to change circumstances.   True.

#38
True
or
False?

Ones: I don't like it when others arbitrarily tell me what to do.

Twos: I usually understand the feelings of others.

Threes: I often have little self-confidence.

Fours: I adapt easily to new situations.

Fives: I rarely get embarrassed.

Sixes: I keep few secrets from people.

Sevens: I am a connoisseur of food and wine.

Eights: I can usually handle tough situations.

Nines: I am sometimes envious of others' success.

#38
Answers

Ones do not like to be arbitrarily controlled, but they like definite rules.   True.

Twos are good at understanding what makes others tick.   True.

Threes usually believe they can successfully finish their tasks.   False.

Fours do not adjust quickly to change.   False.

Fives easily become uncomfortable with others.   False.

Sixes often keep intimate facts about themselves secret from friends.   False.

Sevens often enjoy the pleasures of the palate.   True.

Eights, of all personality types, are most at ease in tough situations.   True.

Nines generally accept their situation and are not envious of others.   False.

#39
True
or
False?

Ones: I am an idealist.

Twos: I don't care if people dislike me.

Threes: I must admit that I am vain.

Fours: I am an elitist.

Fives: I have very few needs.

Sixes: I am rarely serious.

Sevens: I stay away from thrilling or adventurous things.

Eights: I play as hard as I work.

Nines: I plan a lot for the future.

#39
Answers

Ones are idealistic and expect perfection.   True.

Twos usually want everyone to like them.
   False.

Threes usually spend time and energy on their
   image.   True.

Fours can be snobs and prefer to surround
   themselves with others of similar
   interests.   True.

Fives think they have few needs.   True.

Sixes can be too serious and solemn.   False.

Sevens often look for new thrills.   False.

Eights work and play hard, but can also put all
   their energy into play.   True.

Nines usually are not overly concerned with the
   future.   False.

#40
True
or
False?

Ones: I can get annoyed at imperfection in others.

Twos: I am responsible.

Threes: I am sometimes called abrupt.

Fours: I am often very serious.

Fives: I ask for help when I need it.

Sixes: I am faithful to my friends.

Sevens: I prefer to be alone when I am in pain.

Eights: I am honest.

Nines: I sometimes feel bored.

#40
Answers

Ones want others to be perfect.   True.

Twos are usually dependable and keep their word.   True.

Threes can unwittingly be too quick and blunt with others.   True.

Fours can be somber.   True.

Fives usually dislike admitting that they require assistance.   False.

Sixes usually stay loyal in their important relationships.   True.

Sevens tend to withdraw to recover.   True.

Eights have a high sense of integrity.   True.

Nines tend to become bored more frequently than other personality types.   True.

#41
True
or
False?

Ones: I am very honest.

Twos: I am usually gentle.

Threes: I sometimes boast about my success.

Fours: I relate better to individuals than to groups.

Fives: I am open-minded.

Sixes: I am seldom nervous.

Sevens: I seldom daydream.

Eights: I usually don't get involved.

Nines: I rarely forget things.

#41
Answers

Ones usually have integrity and a high moral standard.   True.

Twos usually have an easygoing and considerate personality.   True.

Threes can brag about the good things in their life.   True.

Fours prefer to be with one person at a time. True.

Fives listen to both sides of an issue.   True.

Sixes can be unsure of themselves and therefore nervous.   False.

Sevens like to dream of the next adventure to come.   False.

Eights usually care enough to get involved. False.

Nines can forget many things, especially details. False.

#42
True
or
False?

Ones: I am not very stable.

Twos: I can usually deal with rejection quite well.

Threes: I have no use for titles or awards.

Fours: I am sensitive to the feelings of others.

Fives: I am usually patient.

Sixes: I am rarely shy.

Sevens: I sometimes smile to hide my true feelings.

Eights: I can be shy with strangers.

Nines: I often try to improve myself and my environment.

#42
Answers

Ones are generally stable and dependable.
False.

Twos want to be liked and often find it difficult to deal with rejection.   False.

Threes put stock in public recognition.   False.

Fours usually empathize with others.   True.

Fives usually can wait for what they want.
True.

Sixes, on occasion, can be extremely shy.
False.

Sevens can be uncomfortable with feelings.
True.

Eights usually speak out and assert themselves.
False.

Nines mostly reconcile themselves to the way things are.   False.

#43
True
or
False?

Ones: I am reliable.

Twos: I have empathy for others.

Threes: I am often anxious.

Fours: I appreciate the small things in life.

Fives: I consider myself an original thinker.

Sixes: I easily make decisions.

Sevens: I can be impatient.

Eights: I seldom help others and prefer to remain aloof.

Nines: I sometimes feel that life is a battle.

#43
Answers

Ones can usually be counted on.   True.

Twos usually understand others quite well.
True.

Threes can be anxious about failure.   True.

Fours can take delight in small details that escape
others.   True.

Fives often use their knowledge to discover new
concepts.   True.

Sixes often are uncertain and vacillate.   False.

Sevens dislike waiting around and want immediate
action.   True.

Eights can be generous with their assistance.
False.

Nines sometimes feel battered by the world.
True.

#44
True
or
False?

Ones: I often take the side of the underdog.

Twos: I have, on occasion, been hysterical.

Threes: I view my company's (or group's) success or failure as my own.

Fours: I sometimes freely give my time to a good cause.

Fives: I often don't trust those around me.

Sixes: I easily deal with my inner feelings.

Sevens: I am usually a quiet person.

Eights: I am more sensitive than I allow others to see.

Nines: I believe that I am more important than most others.

#44
Answers

Ones come to the defense of disadvantaged people.   True.

Twos can become hysterical under trying conditions.   True.

Threes take group success or failure personally. True.

Fours can be generous with their time and talents.   True.

Fives protect themselves from others.   True.

Sixes are generally logical but are often not aware of their own feelings.   False.

Sevens usually are lively and talkative.   False.

Eights can be deeply affected by the sufferings of others.   True.

Nines usually are modest and not pompous or pretentious.   False.

#45
True
or
False?

Ones: I am a loyal friend.

Twos: I suffer anxiety.

Threes: I sometimes believe significant results are more important than the individuals concerned.

Fours: I consider myself cultured.

Fives: I am not a very deep thinker.

Sixes: I am usually compassionate.

Sevens: I am aware of the needs of others.

Eights: I sometimes work to make my country a better place.

Nines: I can be an enjoyable companion.

#45
Answers

Ones often demonstrate a sense of loyalty.
True.

Twos worry about the future.   True.

Threes can hold the successful completion of their
task as more important than the people it
affects.   True.

Fours are generally refined people of good
taste.   True.

Fives can be curious and deeply logical about
many things.   False.

Sixes care deeply about those to whom they are
committed.   True.

Sevens often can sense needs in others but may
choose to remain uninvolved.   True.

Eights often work to improve their country, city, or
neighborhood.   True.

Nines usually are comfortable to be with because
they make few demands on their
friends.   True.

#46
True
or
False?

Ones: I often feel guilty.

Twos: I can be a romantic.

Threes: I sometimes might be a bit aggressive.

Fours: I enjoy good health.

Fives: I am loyal to my friends.

Sixes: I respect older and wiser people.

Sevens: I am more serious than most people.

Eights: I am in control of my life.

Nines: I am a gentle caring person.

#46
Answers

Ones can sometimes feel guilty for no real reason.   True.

Twos can be sentimental.   True.

Threes can try to dominate.   True.

Fours can go through much suffering.   False.

Fives are usually faithful to the few commitments they make.   True.

Sixes regard leaders or elders with much esteem.   True.

Sevens like to have fun and don't take things too seriously.   False.

Eights work hard to be in control of everything that affects them.   True.

Nines generally are kind, soothing people.   True.

#47
True
or
False?

Ones: I rarely object to others' behavior.

Twos: I've been known to be controlling.

Threes: I sometimes encourage others to improve themselves.

Fours: I am often misunderstood.

Fives: I often help others.

Sixes: I am often stressed.

Sevens: I consider myself a jack-of-all-trades.

Eights: I usually say it like it is, even if this upsets others.

Nines: I confront those who don't see things my way.

#47
Answers

Ones are often critical of the behavior of others. False.

Twos may try to control others by being of help to them.   True.

Threes can spark improvement in others.   True.

Fours often believe others do not understand them.   True.

Fives would rather remain observers and not get involved.   False.

Sixes can get anxious over group and personal relationships.   True.

Sevens are often accomplished at many things. True.

Eights can be abrasive and tactless.   True.

Nines try to avoid conflict.   False.

#48
True
or
False?

Ones: I go with the flow.

Twos: I can be physically violent.

Threes: I use debate and persuasion effectively.

Fours: I have a tastefully decorated home.

Fives: I belong to a number of clubs or groups.

Sixes: I sometimes playfully tease my close friends.

Sevens: I tend to put off doing unpleasant tasks.

Eights: I am often concerned about issues involving justice.

Nines: I am generally a well-balanced person.

#48
Answers

Ones see a lot wrong with the world and strive to correct it.   False.

Twos are generally nonviolent.   False.

Threes can be quite persuasive in getting their way.   True.

Fours are often artists at heart and like to surround themselves with beauty.   True.

Fives usually do not regularly participate in groups or organizations.   False.

Sixes can be jovial and humorous with their few close friends.   True.

Sevens often delay doing disagreeable things.   True.

Eights usually want life to be fair.   True.

Nines usually are the most balanced of the personality types.   True.

#49
True
or
False?

Ones: I seldom explain my position on an issue.

Twos: I get close to my friends.

Threes: I don't like to join groups.

Fours: I am a happy person most of the time.

Fives: I usually speak softly.

Sixes: I honor tradition.

Sevens: I like group gatherings.

Eights: I do not like to yield to others.

Nines: I can overreact to a minor emergency.

#49
Answers

Ones can forcefully debate their point of
  view.   False.

Twos get close to people they like.   True.

Threes usually find group participation important.
  False.

Fours are generally not jubilant people.   False.

Fives normally do not talk loudly.   True.

Sixes willingly follow the customs and practices of
  their groups.   True.

Sevens usually like to be with people who are
  having fun.   True.

Eights do not like giving up.   True.

Nines are seldom upset by minor
  emergencies.   False.

#50
True
or
False?

Ones: I often lose my temper.

Twos: I can flatter others.

Threes: I probably wouldn't win a popularity contest.

Fours: I rarely complain.

Fives: I am a warm, friendly person.

Sixes: I encourage my friends to be all they can be.

Sevens: I am at times very talkative.

Eights: I take care of my family and friends.

Nines: I welcome most people, even if they are different from myself.

#50
Answers

Ones feel anger, but it is usually a cold, unemotional anger.   False.

Twos are often good at the art of flattery. True.

Threes are popular with others.   False.

Fours can have difficulty accepting things as they are.   False.

Fives are usually rather cold in their interactions with others.   False.

Sixes can inspire their friends to greater achievement.   True.

Sevens talk a lot and sometimes talk so much they forget to listen to others.   True.

Eights usually protect and care for their friends. True.

Nines are not often judgmental of others and accept differences.   True.

True or False Score Sheet

Ones	Twos	Threes	Fours	Fives	Sixes	Sevens	Eights	Nines
1.___	1.___	1.___	1.___	1.___	1.___	1.___	1.___	1.___
2.___	2.___	2.___	2.___	2.___	2.___	2.___	2.___	2.___
3.___	3.___	3.___	3.___	3.___	3.___	3.___	3.___	3.___
4.___	4.___	4.___	4.___	4.___	4.___	4.___	4.___	4.___
5.___	5.___	5.___	5.___	5.___	5.___	5.___	5.___	5.___
6.___	6.___	6.___	6.___	6.___	6.___	6.___	6.___	6.___
7.___	7.___	7.___	7.___	7.___	7.___	7.___	7.___	8.___
8.___	8.___	8.___	8.___	8.___	8.___	8.___	8.___	8.___
9.___	9.___	9.___	9.___	9.___	9.___	9.___	9.___	9.___
10.___	10.___	10.___	10.___	10.___	10.___	10.___	10.___	10.___
11.___	11.___	11.___	11.___	11.___	11.___	11.___	11.___	11.___
12.___	12.___	12.___	12.___	12.___	12.___	12.___	12.___	12.___
13.___	13.___	13.___	13.___	13.___	13.___	13.___	13.___	13.___
14.___	14.___	14.___	14.___	14.___	14.___	14.___	14.___	14.___
15.___	15.___	15.___	15.___	15.___	15.___	15.___	15.___	15.___
16.___	16.___	16.___	16.___	16.___	16.___	16.___	16.___	16.___
17.___	17.___	17.___	17.___	17.___	17.___	17.___	17.___	17.___
18.___	18.___	18.___	18.___	18.___	18.___	18.___	18.___	18.___
19.___	19.___	19.___	19.___	19.___	19.___	19.___	19.___	19.___
20.___	20.___	20.___	20.___	20.___	20.___	20.___	20.___	20.___
21.___	21.___	21.___	21.___	21.___	21.___	21.___	21.___	21.___
22.___	22.___	22.___	22.___	22.___	22.___	22.___	22.___	22.___
23.___	23.___	23.___	23.___	23.___	23.___	23.___	23.___	23.___
24.___	24.___	24.___	24.___	24.___	24.___	24.___	24.___	24.___
25.___	25.___	25.___	25.___	25.___	25.___	25.___	25.___	25.___
26.___	26.___	26.___	26.___	26.___	26.___	26.___	26.___	26.___
27.___	27.___	27.___	27.___	27.___	27.___	27.___	27.___	27.___
28.___	28.___	28.___	28.___	28.___	28.___	28.___	28.___	28.___
29.___	29.___	29.___	29.___	29.___	29.___	29.___	29.___	29.___
30.___	30.___	30.___	30.___	30.___	30.___	30.___	30.___	30.___
31.___	31.___	31.___	31.___	31.___	31.___	31.___	31.___	31.___
32.___	32.___	32.___	32.___	32.___	32.___	32.___	32.___	32.___
33.___	33.___	33.___	33.___	33.___	33.___	33.___	33.___	33.___
34.___	34.___	34.___	34.___	34.___	34.___	34.___	34.___	34.___
35.___	35.___	35.___	35.___	35.___	35.___	35.___	35.___	35.___
36.___	36.___	36.___	36.___	36.___	36.___	36.___	36.___	36.___
37.___	37.___	37.___	37.___	37.___	37.___	37.___	37.___	37.___
38.___	38.___	38.___	38.___	38.___	38.___	38.___	38.___	38.___
39.___	39.___	39.___	39.___	39.___	39.___	39.___	39.___	39.___
40.___	40.___	40.___	40.___	40.___	40.___	40.___	40.___	40.___
41.___	41.___	41.___	41.___	41.___	41.___	41.___	41.___	41.___
42.___	42.___	42.___	42.___	42.___	42.___	42.___	42.___	42.___
43.___	43.___	43.___	43.___	43.___	43.___	43.___	43.___	43.___
44.___	44.___	44.___	44.___	44.___	44.___	44.___	44.___	44.___
45.___	45.___	45.___	45.___	45.___	45.___	45.___	45.___	45.___
46.___	46.___	46.___	46.___	46.___	46.___	46.___	46.___	46.___
47.___	47.___	47.___	47.___	47.___	47.___	47.___	47.___	47.___
48.___	48.___	48.___	48.___	48.___	48.___	48.___	48.___	48.___
49.___	49.___	49.___	49.___	49.___	49.___	49.___	49.___	49.___
50.___	50.___	50.___	50.___	50.___	50.___	50.___	50.___	50.___
SCORE	SCORE	SCORE	SCORE	SCORE	SCORE	SCORE	SCORE	SCORE

Interpreting Your Results from the Score Sheet

After you have scored a check or zero or left a blank for each of the fifty true or false statements for a personality type, award yourself points according to the following system:

Check: 2

Zero: 0

Blank: 1

On the score sheet, enter your total point score at the bottom of the column for that personality type. The highest score indicates your enneagram personality type.

If the difference between your highest and next highest scores is less than six points, the results are inconclusive. In this case, you should read through the rest of this book as background and then take the True or False Test again.

Part Three

The Personality Types

5

Occupations, Interactions, Problems, and Personal Growth

No single enneagram personality type is better than another. All nine personality types have their positive and negative aspects. Certainly, nothing in the tests you have taken is intended to pass judgment on anyone. What the tests can do for you is make you more aware of your strengths and weaknesses. Once you recognize them, you are in a better position to make allowances for yourself where you do not have great strength, and to take advantage of those areas in which you are more capable or confident than most people.

For each enneagram personality type, certain occupations are more congenial. Anyone can work in any occupation, but some jobs are more of a stretch and needlessly stressful for some personality types. In this chapter, we look at the kinds of work for which the nine personality types are most suited and unsuited.

Likewise, anyone can get along with anyone else, but some personality types interact more easily with others. You naturally relate well with certain personality types, and these people most easily become your friends or partners. People who belong to personality types other than these require more effort on your part for closer and satisfying relationships. Knowing another person's enneagram personality type can go far in explaining either the good or bad feelings that exist between you and him or her. The other personality types with which you are most likely to get along are given in this chapter.

Problems are often a matter of how you perceive life. Something that causes one person major anxiety can be regarded by another as a minor annoyance or even a challenge. Your enneagram personality type is often responsible for how you look at things—whether you see a person or an event as pleasant, unpleasant, or neutral. The things most likely to arise as problems in your life are discussed in this chapter according to personality type.

A healthy life is dynamic, never static. When we are really living our lives to the fullest, we are always growing and changing, even when we do not realize it. The indications of active personal growth are given for each enneagram personality type.

Ones

Occupations. Ones have difficulty with work involving many different conflicting ideas, such as being a judge or producer.

Ones excel in positions requiring skill and precise and correct ways of doing the job, for example, as a physician, nurse, clergyman, teacher, accountant, technician, librarian, or secretary.

Interactions. Ones get along easiest with other Ones, Twos, Fours, Sevens, Eights, and Nines.

Problems. Ones are upset by people who are sloppy about their work or appearance. They are easily annoyed by those who ridicule or criticize them.

Ones tend to believe they are the only people who can

do anything right. Consequently, they resent others whose performance does not meet their high standards. They can become judgmental, unwilling to be wrong, and involved in conflicts. Often Ones are unable to express their feelings, and they withhold these feelings instead of dealing with them.

When life presents difficulties—at home or at work—Ones feel misunderstood and tend to be depressed and to withdraw from others. They can feel lost and suffer from self-hate.

Personal Growth. As a One, you know you are growing as a person when:

- You are less concerned with perfection and more interested in what enjoyment you can find in life.

- You are less critical of others and their mistakes, and more aware of the contributions of others.

- You are more relaxed and less stern.

- You are more aware of your own worth and less critical of yourself.

- You are less serious and self-attacking, and more playful.

- You are more truthful and more willing to express feelings.

- You are more aware that the world is perfect just as it is, and less apt to try to change it.

- You are less impatient with life, and more willing to go one step at a time.

- You feel it's less important to pretend to be happy if you're really angry, and accept more things as they are.

Last Word. Ones need to keep in mind that the world is progressing just as it should. The world will never be perfect, nor indeed is it desirable for it to be perfect. Life is not perfect, but is a process of growing day by day. Life need not be serious all the time—it can be relaxing and fun!

Twos

Occupations. Twos are not suited to professions with a high risk of disapproval or loss of popularity, such as politics or law enforcement.

Twos do well in positions requiring sympathy and warmth, for example, as a social worker, psychologist, physician, nurse, executive secretary, or clergyman.

Interactions. Twos get on best with other Twos, Ones, Threes, Fours, Fives, and Eights.

Problems. Twos are upset by people who do not need their help, and they resent people who cause them to feel that they are intruding on their privacy. They dislike being ignored or disregarded, and hate being unneeded.

Twos tend to believe that they themselves do not have needs, and so they often project their real needs onto other people and then try to help them. In the process, Twos may feel they are victims of life. They want people to think of them as helpful and loving, but all the while they are attempting to manipulate others, who may therefore resent them.

If they become mentally unhealthy, Twos often want vengeance. They may become aggressive or, if unable to actually confront their ''enemies,'' develop physical or further mental sickness in order to get needed attention from others.

Personal Growth. As a Two, you are experiencing personal growth when:

- You are depending less on others for your self-esteem and more on yourself.

- You have a more simple life.

- You help people less in the expectation of something in return and more in a spirit of altruism.

- You acknowledge more your own needs, and are less concerned with the needs of others.

- You are less self-deprecating and more self-accepting.
- You manipulate others less with flattery, and become more aware of flattery as a method of control.
- You seek the approval of others less, and give support more with no strings attached.

Last Word. Twos need to recognize their hidden needs and feelings, especially their negative feelings. They should remember that they are important in themselves and not because of what they do for others.

Threes

Occupations. Threes do not feel comfortable with employment that requires a socially unpopular viewpoint, such as a criminal lawyer or worker for a protest group.

Threes have excellent management skills, meaning they can convince others to do things. Among the jobs they enjoy are acting, medicine, marketing, sales, promotion, advertising, corporate management, banking, entrepreneurship, and politics.

Interactions. Threes interact best with other Threes, Twos, Fours, Sixes, and Nines.

Problems. Threes become upset with people who find fault with their work or who say they don't work hard enough.

Threes get multiple tasks completed efficiently, but they have difficulty dealing with negative results. They compulsively avoid even the possibility of failure or anything else that makes them look bad in front of others.

When things don't work out, Threes get out of touch with their feelings and become either hostile or lazy, spaced out, and robotlike.

Personal Growth. You know you are growing as a Three when:

- You are less concerned with being in control, and more willing to trust the world to operate efficiently on its own.
- You are less competitive and more cooperative.
- You are more truthful and less boasting.
- You are less vain and concerned about status.
- You are more self-assured, and less afraid of failure.
- You are more authentic, and less influenced by others.
- You are less superficial and pragmatic (if it works, it's truth), and more focused on enduring character and integrity.
- You are more interested in self-improvement and looking inward (for example, meditation), and less competitive with others.
- You look less for attention and praise.
- You replace personal happiness with long working hours less, and have more satisfaction and happiness in the present moment.

Last Word. Threes need to go beyond their fear of failure by committing themselves to a group or cause they believe is of greater importance than themselves. They should realize that they can't do everything alone, and that others can do some things better. They need to remember that the end never justifies the means.

Fours

Occupations. Fours do not like jobs that make them feel like a small cog in the wheel or that in any way remind them they are not unique, such as in a low-level position.

Fours are creative and do well in the arts, for example, in acting, dancing, painting, and interior decoration. They also do well as critics, entertainers, and counselors.

Interactions. Fours relate most easily with other Fours, Ones, Twos, Threes, and Fives.

Problems. Fours overreact to criticism and, when they are into their suffering moods, dislike people who do not take them seriously. They like to exaggerate or dramatize their life experiences in order to make themselves seem more interesting. They don't like feeling ordinary and try to set themselves apart from others. Consequently they feel isolated and lacking in authenticity. Fours have difficulty with intimate relationships, and spend time in fantasy instead of action.

When things do not go their way, Fours often become morbid and try to attach themselves to people. Because they are more concerned at such times with what other people think of them, their fear of rejection is increased. At their worst, they can become emotionally blocked and self-destructive through drugs or even suicide.

Personal Growth. Your life is evolving in a healthy way as a Four when:

- You feel less self-pity and envy of others, and realize more the oneness of all life.

- You feel less trapped in your own emotional life, and more creative.

- You procrastinate less, and act more.

- You are more diligent and hardworking, and feel less like sabotaging projects.

- You act more instinctively, and think less about feelings.

- You feel less pressure to be special, and accept more the way things are.

- You are more assertive, and feel less like a victim.

- You think less about your idealized self, and more about your real self.

Last Word. Fours need not take everything so personally, and should discipline themselves to accomplish tasks, regardless of their ever-changing moods. They should recognize that they are part of humanity and that they are not unique and different in every area. It would do them no harm to remember that happiness consists of accepting things as they are and not wanting them to be different.

Fives

Occupations. The jobs that Fives find stressful are those with high visibility, such as a television reporter, and those in which their boss can determine exactly how well they do each day, as in sales.

Fives excel in positions that need logical thinking, such as accountant, computer programmer, writer, librarian, research scientist, archaeologist, or other academic position.

Interactions. Fives have their most easily satisfying relationships with other Fives, Twos, Fours, Sixes, and Eights.

Problems. Fives get upset with pushy people who make demands on them. They often accumulate knowledge in order to fill their empty lives. Feeling despair and withdrawing from others, they can become mere observers of life instead of true participants.

If life gets tough, Fives believe they should plan their way out of trouble but daydream instead of following through on their plans. They may become antagonistic toward those who are critical of their dreams or beliefs. They may identify with radical causes or ideas, and can become paranoid and frightened.

Personal Growth. You know you are moving onward and upward as a Five when:

• You are less stingy, and more willing to share with others.

- You observe life less, and live it more.
- You are more assertive, and less afraid to use power.
- You are less intense, and more relaxed.
- You hoard less, and give to others more willingly.
- You have a "We can do it" attitude and cooperate more with others, and are less of a loner.
- You are less of an intellectual snob and more willing to pass what you know on to others.
- You are more compassionate, and less judgmental of emotional people.
- You think more originally, and rely less on storing learned facts.
- You are more willing to present yourself as an active player in life, and less as a minimal participant.

Last Word. Fives need to replace their insecurity with the confidence that comes from believing that they are, in fact, knowledgeable enough to live bravely in reality with the rest of humanity.

Sixes

Occupations. Positions that involve serious judgment calls, such as those of judge or doctor, create great tensions for Sixes, as do jobs that involve under-the-table manipulations or highly competitive environments.

Sixes do best where logical methods exist for determining the correct course of action, for example, as a school instructor, engineer, officer in the armed forces, police officer, firefighter, civil servant, machinist, builder, or technologist.

Interactions. Sixes require less effort to get along with other Sixes, Threes, Fives, Sevens, and Nines.

Problems. Sixes react negatively to people who see things differently or who appear to be feebleminded.

Sixes tend to run from their fears and seek security in the family or a group. They dislike deviations from group ethics that might threaten the group and therefore their security.

In times of adversity, Sixes tend to be increasingly anxious about how they appear to others. They feel more incompetent, seem unable to act on their own, and complain more about their problems. Sixes can become self-destructive or become aggressive toward others when mentally unhealthy.

Personal Growth. Your personal growth as a Six is progressing well when:

- You pay less attention to self-doubt and trust yourself more.
- You are less anxious, and more self-assured.
- You are less defensive, and more trusting of others.
- You do less talking or thinking, and more feeling or intuiting.
- You are more comfortable with life, and less cynical.
- You think less in terms of black and white, and more in shades of gray.
- You are more responsible, and less indecisive.
- You have more faith in the positive progress of life.

Last Word. Sixes need to overcome their fear of being different from their peers, and become more independent. They need the courage to risk new things instead of doing the same old things repeatedly.

Sevens

Occupations. Sevens have difficulty with routine employment (such as that of a factory worker), where they have to take care of the details while they are controlled by a supervisor who does all the planning for them.

Sevens are most at home in positions that necessitate

planning or researching new concepts. They are better in staff jobs than line jobs. Suggested jobs and fields include consultant, editor, management staff, sales, public relations, entrepreneur, writer, and scientist.

Interactions. Sevens naturally relate well to other Sevens, Ones, Fives, Sixes, and Eights.

Problems. Sevens get riled by people who try to force or manipulate them to do things that aren't fun.

Sevens like to make many plans but actually carry out few of them. They dream rather than do the work necessary for their plans to reach fruition.

When life deals Sevens a poor hand, they tend to be resentful, lose their usual optimism, and find fault with things. They may become rude and aggressive, or try to forget their anxieties through sex, drink, drugs, or food. When giving up one vice or bad habit, they often substitute another.

Personal Growth. Your life as a Seven is flourishing when:

- You give less importance to the pursuit of pleasure, and more to sobriety and awareness of the moment.
- You are doing less planning, and achieving more work and production.
- You are less concerned with amount, and more concerned with quality.
- You see life not solely as pleasure, but as a mixture of joy and pain.
- You do less getting, and more giving.
- You are less desperate to be happy at any cost, and more willing to experience unhappiness.
- You are less dependent on being with others, and more willing to just observe and know.
- You feel less deprived, and more satisfied with life as it is.

- You are less impulsive, and more willing to wait for things.

- You recognize daydreams as mere diversions, and don't avoid real feelings and experiences.

Last Word. Sevens need to stop running away from painful reality and realize that life contains both pain and pleasure. They should be willing to follow through on their plans, even when this is difficult and painful. They need to take life as it is, without trying to sweeten it or escape it.

Eights

Occupations. Eights have a lot of difficulty with jobs like those in factories, where they are the underdogs who must follow orders, and are not in a position of power.

Eights excel in positions where they have a lot of power, for example, as a commissioned or noncommissioned officer in the armed forces, police officer, attorney, sports figure, businessman, union organizer, and business manager.

Interactions. Eights achieve the most easygoing interactions with other Eights, Ones, Twos, Fives, Sevens, and Nines.

Problems. Eights have no time for weak people who won't stand up for themselves. They are often champions of justice or law and order. Denying they have any weaknesses, they scare others with their tough exterior.

When they are disappointed, Eights often withdraw and become introverted. They become stingy with their money, time, and help for others, and may cheat or lie. Mentally unhealthy Eights can be paranoid and physically dangerous.

Personal Growth. You are moving along under full sail as an Eight when:

- You see life less in simple black-and-white terms.

- You try less to make life fair and just, and accept it more as it is.
- You are less macho and tough, and more tender and vulnerable.
- You have more power, but also more self-restraint over that power.
- You are less self-centered, and more caring for others.
- You are more liked, and less feared by others.
- You have less concern about money, and more about family and friends.
- You are more a leader of others, but more helpful and less aggressive toward them.
- You are more willing to see other people's point of view, and less obsessed with being right.

Last Word. Eights have to remember not to use their power to control others, but instead realize that others have rights. They should guide others and work in a spirit of cooperation and openness. Eights need to drop or soften their hard outer shell.

Nines

Occupations. Nines have difficulty in jobs that require a bold statement, such as a fashion model, or that require quick movement from one situation to another, such as a quarterback, or that require self-promotion, as in sales.

Nines are most contented where they can perform routine work with a lot of structure or where they can act as a peacemaker between conflicting sides. They are suited to the position of arbitrator, ambassador, administrator, bureaucrat, and umpire or referee, and also do well in public relations and at detail work in a laboratory or manufacturing plant.

Interactions. Nines get along most easily with other Nines, Ones, Threes, Sixes, and Eights.

Problems. Nines are upset by people who regularly cause conflict. Seeking harmony at any cost, they can even ignore reality in an effort to deny the existence of conflict. This often results in laziness.

When events go badly for Nines, they experience self-doubt and have even more difficulty making decisions. They can be resistant to change and withdraw from life, and they can become depressed and think that life is too demanding and dangerous.

Personal Growth. As a Nine, you are correct in your belief that you are developing as a person when:

- You withdraw less, and become more active in the pursuit of life.

- You have less problem setting deadlines and timetables, and are more successful in business and life.

- You procrastinate less, and act more.

- You become more of a self-starter and take an increased interest in life.

- You see love less as a selfish, private thing, and more as something which binds us all together.

- You are more supportive of friends, but less dependent on others.

- You are more conscious of the moment, and daydream less.

- You are less concerned with the eventual goal, and more fixed on the present reality.

- You are less lazy, and exercise more.

Last Word. Nines need to be more flexible and accept change. They can increase their flexibility by learning new ways of expressing their feelings, even if this upsets others. They also need to put their natural abilities to more use, thereby raising their self-esteem.

6

Personality Strengths

Who hasn't listened to well-meant advice about getting to know our own weaknesses? We are advised much less often to get to know our own strengths, which is at as least as—if not more—important than getting to know our weaknesses. We are talking here, of course, about emotional strength, the invisible thing in us to which other people respond, often unconsciously.

Emotional strength can make a personality forceful or gentle. There are no muscles to flex or biceps to measure. All the same, the presence of emotional strength in someone can be just as intimidating as obvious physical strength. And its absence in a person is much more weakening than a mere lack of muscles.

By knowing our own weaknesses, we can avoid areas in which we are particularly vulnerable. By knowing our strengths, we can increase our efforts when we recognize ourselves to be in a strong position and thereby maximize our returns. These may be psychic returns, such as affection or tranquillity, or physical returns, such as hard cash or good health. This chapter deals more with the psychic returns. It is not about how to get rich or keep fit—at least not directly, although people in good emotional health are most liable to earn high incomes and feel well physically.

The strengths of each of the nine enneagram personality types are presented in numerical order.

Ones

Ones do the right thing. They are not easily influenced by social pressures if these go against what they think is right. Not overly concerned whether others like or dislike what they do, they act according to their own values.

Mature Ones have an aura of emotional calm about them—a kind of tranquillity or sense of being at ease with themselves.

All Ones are careful and good at tasks that do not necessitate speed. Their sense of humor is liable to be like that of Johnny Carson. And they generally dig in and hold their ground on any matter of principle.

Twos

Twos are very sensitive to various emotional levels. They know what other people are feeling and recognize what they really want. But theirs is not a case of empathy only—they are willing to take care of others, and are very good at it.

They often have a charming silliness and playfulness in the style of Goldie Hawn.

Twos know how to impress others. Generally they know how to get people to like them, although this may not be something they care about one way or the other.

Threes

Threes are goal-oriented. They give themselves a job to do or set themselves a mark to attain, and give it one hundred percent of their effort. It hardly needs to be said that they work hard.

They mix well with other people, in just about any group that they care to choose.

Threes know how to look good. They have an awareness of how they as individuals are seen by other people, and an innate gift of knowing how to present themselves to the world.

Fours

Fours have a highly developed artistic sense. They are likely to have one or more talents in almost any field, for example, acting, painting, singing, and writing.

On the other hand, they are deeply in touch with the pain and sadness of existence.

Fours really know how to make an entrance or exit. They know what dramatic effect is and how to use it. Their sense of style and fashion is keen, and they don't hesitate to express themselves as individuals.

Fives

Fives have a good sense of objectivity. Aware of the value of things, and the limitations of time and money, they use the resources at their disposal efficiently.

They are good conversationalists. And they can be good listeners too. Mostly they do not rock the boat or stir up trouble.

Fives are independent and don't look to others to take care of them. This streak of independence makes them good at solo work and even permits them to operate in isolation.

Sixes

Sixes have a long attention span. Their ability to concentrate allows them to undertake things that would drive the rest of us crazy because of the carefulness and precision required. They are good at planning and implementing strategies.

Sixes are adventuresome and take risks. They can be rebellious in a positive way, by questioning and standing up to authority. They are the ones most likely to confront other people with an opposing point of view.

Sevens

Sevens don't have many personal problems. Generally they are social, easy to get along with, and pleasant—even charming. They can be intellectuals.

Sevens have dreams and visions of what's possible. They are idea people and imaginative brainstormers. Theirs is a positive, upbeat approach to life. Often they have discriminating tastes in food, clothing, and many other areas.

Eights

With Eights, what you see is what you get. Eights really let people know where they stand. They have no problem in confronting life.

They can be loyal, devoted friends. In general, they are not practical jokers or mischievous, and are defenders of the weak.

Beneath their hard outer shell, Eights are gentle and empathetic.

Nines

Nines are good at seeing all sides of an issue. They can make quick decisions. They don't hesitate to call a ball or a strike—and usually they make the right call without thinking much about it.

Nines have big hearts. Fairly generous and easygoing, they are there for others and don't expect anything in return.

7

Personality Types of Famous People

None of the celebrities mentioned here took the tests in this book, so assigning them to particular enneagram personality types involved a certain amount of educated and—we hope—inspired guesswork. The greatest potential for error is contained in the amount by which a celebrity's authentic private personality differs from his or her public image. These personality type assignments were made solely according to public image—indeed, a few are of fictional characters.

It is possible that if we knew more about the real characteristics of some of these prominent people, we would assign them to a different personality type. However, it's reasonable to believe that the public image associated with a person is not there by accident, and that it does provide some kind of window into that person's soul. Dolly Parton and Henry Kissinger might strike you differently if you could only see them, without their knowledge, relaxing at home. But how different would they be? Not totally different, that's almost certain.

Ones

Nancy Reagan
Johnny Carson
Jacqueline Onassis
Dr. Jekyll
   (Mr. Hyde is an Eight)

Barbara Walters
Audrey Hepburn
Tom Smothers
Confucius
Ann Landers

Twos

Dolly Parton
Goldie Hawn
Jerry Lewis
Elton John

Marilyn Monroe
Elvis Presley
Sally Field

Threes

John F. Kennedy
Arnold Schwarzenegger
Doris Day
Werner Erhart
Bill Clinton

Jimmy Carter
Donald Trump
Wolfgang Amadeus
   Mozart
Robert Redford

Fours

Cher
Edgar Allen Poe
Scarlett O'Hara
Gloria Steinem
Mary Hartman
Brian Ferry
Alan Watts

Bette Davis
Neil Young
Daniel Day Lewis
Vanessa Redgrave
Joni Mitchell
Leslie Howard

Fives

Henry Fonda
Emily Dickinson
Frederic Chopin
Howard Hughes

Henry Kissinger
Thomas Edison
Buddha

Sixes

Woody Allen
Richard Nixon
Sigmund Freud
George Bush

Hamlet
Sonny Bono
Krishnamurti

Sevens

Bill Cosby
Carl Sagan
Kurt Vonnegut

Loni Anderson
Alan Alda
Henry David Thoreau

Eights

Ludwig van Beethoven
Bette Midler
Zorba the Greek
Henry VIII
Mr. T
Marlon Brando

General George Patton
Pablo Picasso
Joan Rivers
Danny DeVito
Joseph Stalin
Charles Bronson

Nines

Barbara Bush
Lyndon B. Johnson
Gerald Ford
Julia Child

Jean Stapleton
Hubert Humphrey
Alfred Hitchcock

8

How They Talk and What They Say

It's reasonable to assume that people who have many emotional things in common—that is, those who belong to a particular enneagram personality type—will also resemble each other in how they communicate. What they have to say, and how they say it, can be a valuable guide as to whether they are Ones or Eights or whatever. Indeed, if you listen to people long enough, they often end up inadvertently answering many of the test questions in this book, perhaps enough for you to make a reliable judgment of their personality type.

Here are the ways that the nine enneagram personality types typically, but not always, communicate.

Ones

Ones like to complain about what's wrong. They are angry about it, and not at all resigned. You may also find that they do not hesitate to tell you what to do for your own good.

Twos

Twos like to talk about themselves, their personal problems, and public issues they regard as important. They are also willing to talk about your problems. Notice how they often hold eye contact with you while they talk.

Threes

Threes love to talk about the great things that are going on in their life. They're big on selling themselves, and will try to enroll you in doing what they are doing.

Fours

Fours complain in a resigned way. They tell you all about their problems and the drama in their life. But you find that they are cleverly analytical about their emotions and motives, and those of other people.

Fives

Fives say as little as possible. They communicate about facts and information in a detached way, without emotional involvement. Their stories can be long.

Sixes

Sixes argue with you on an analytical level. They caution you to take heed of various dangers.

Sevens

Sevens have friendly, agreeable discussions. They are good storytellers and get you involved in personal narratives. Not concentrating much on feelings, they are better at discussing plans and theories on an intellectual or abstract level.

Eights

Eights are direct in what they say and the way they say it. They may or may not use earthy language. In an arrogant way, they often complain about people who don't come up to their standards.

Nines

Nines like to listen to talk about what is happening to other people. They go in for a kind of resigned complaining (not the angry or arrogant complaining of a One or an Eight). Usually they are not really upset, yet can sound a little depressed.

9

Gentle Persuasion

You hear people talk of pressing other people's emotional buttons, electronic age lingo for the ancient art of persuasion or seduction. Each of the nine enneagram personality types is susceptible to particular kinds of emotional manipulation. This need not always be interpreted in the injurious sense, since the emotional manipulation may be benevolent, undertaken by someone who cares deeply.

We all—even the strongest and most independent—have our areas of emotional vulnerability, and those who wish to affect us most deeply, out of either love or hate, can do so most easily by probing these regions. But this does not always have to be at a profound level. For example, a little flattery where it counts can be all that's needed to clinch some minor business transaction—or get you invited somewhere you are curious to see.

Here is a quick guide to the ways in which each enneagram personality type, including your own, can most easily be persuaded.

Ones

You can flatter Ones by asking them questions and treating their answers respectfully. They like to teach and have their opinion sought. You can break the ice with a One by telling a tasteful joke.

Twos

More than any other personality type, Twos love affection. They seek your approval and want your validation. Pat them on the back and let them know they are liked or loved for who they are. Once they know they are needed, they will do things for you, as long as you show recognition and appreciation.

Threes

Threes enjoy being admired for how happy and successful they look. All you have to do is applaud them for their beauty and achievements.

Fours

Fours know how unique and special they are. They will especially enjoy your compliments on their esthetic taste. Your continued support, compliments, and friendship, particularly during times when they are saying nasty things about you, are deeply appreciated, as is your sympathy when they are suffering.

Fives

Fives want you, and everyone else, to be impressed with their vast knowledge and in awe of their wisdom. Take it from there.

Sixes

Let Sixes know you respect them because they are creative, intelligent, loyal, and sexy.

Sevens

Sevens want you to experience the good things in life with them. Unfortunately, this includes participating in their many dreams and plans for the future.

Eights

Be open and honest with Eights. Speak up for yourself. They will be the ones asking you how they can help.

Nines

Nines are flattered if you pay them attention and include them as central people in your activities. Nines like to help you, but don't expect anything in return for their help.

10

Personality Types that Can Be Confused

Certain enneagram personality types can be confused with others. This occurs because the members of the two groups share some similar characteristics. In many cases, the characteristics are most similar at first glance—and seem less so when looked at more closely.

Here are the six likeliest combinations to cause confusion, and reliable ways to tell them apart.

Ones and Fives

Fives are more involved in internal control, while Ones care more about outer control, such as over other people and over things. Fives look inward; Ones look outward.

Ones and Sixes

Sixes are more concerned with keeping safe, while Ones are involved in making things right. Both have many rules, but Sixes have safety rules and Ones have rectifying rules. Sixes are more likely to be rebellious, and Ones more likely to be neat and tidy.

Twos and Nines

Twos have more pride, try harder to be pleasing to others, and more often expect something in return for what they give. Nines are more amiable and friendly, but they also are less likely to make an effort to impress.

Threes and Sevens

Threes don't like to spend much time in thought and are more inclined toward action. Sevens are more concerned with keeping the mind stimulated. In addition, Threes care far more than Sevens about success and status symbols.

Threes and Eights

Threes are more concerned with their image. Eights are brassier and not so worried about how others see them. Threes are smooth and charming; Eights are confrontational.

Fours and Sevens

Fours are more inclined to be emotional, even saddened by personal problems. Sevens are more theoretical and logical.

11

Hidden Fears

Many people who make a fortune claim they were not driven by greed for money or power, but by fear of poverty. Our fears are often every bit as strong as our desires—and just as irrational.

We hide our ambitions from other people (and sometimes from ourselves). So, too, we hide our fears. With good reason, because when you know a person's secret fear, you may know his or her greatest weakness.

All of us share feelings of fear about certain things, for example, a car hurtling toward us out of control. Some of us have fears, called phobias, about things that we realize are harmless, such as moths. We are not talking about phobias here, but about the kinds of fear that everyone has to some degree. Therefore, when we say that a person has a hidden fear of something, we mean he or she has a stronger than normal fear of it. Rather than the presence or absence of fear, we are referring to the amount of fear he or she feels.

These hidden fears are stronger than normal fears, yet they usually don't qualify as full-fledged mental problems that cause disruptions in everyday life, apart from being responsible for occasional bad dreams. However, these fears do cause what is called avoidance behavior. This means that, to some extent, people with the fear do certain things solely to avoid circumstances that arouse the fear in them.

People of each personality type tend to share a characteristic hidden fear, and they also tend to behave in a similar way to avoid arousing this fear. Here's how the enneagram personalities resist their nightmare situations.

Ones

Ones fear boiling over in anger. Instead, they tend to be cold and resentful, leaving their anger unresolved.

Twos

Twos fear having personal needs. Instead, they take care of the needs of others.

Threes

Threes fear failure and disgrace. Instead, they get comfort by identifying with success.

Fours

Fours fear having average or commonplace lives. Instead, they embellish their lives so that they seem to be unique to others.

Fives

Fives fear lives without meaning and structure. Instead, they fill their empty moments with facts and learning.

Sixes

Sixes fear separation or rejection from their families, friends, and coworkers. Instead, they are loyal and careful to avoid disapproval.

Sevens

Sevens fear pain and suffering. Instead, they plan ahead carefully to avoid pain and focus on pleasant things.

Eights

Eights fear weakness in themselves. Instead, they become powerful and stand up for themselves and others.

Nines

Nines fear conflict and strife. Instead, they seek harmony and peace at any price.

12

Physical Appearances

The physical appearances of the enneagram personality types are not as reliable a guide as the emotional characteristics. Indeed, some people refuse to take them seriously at all. You might keep this in mind if some of the physical descriptions do not fit in well with other personality data about yourself or someone else. And, as always, some people are exceptions to the rule. Additionally, these are descriptions of Americans, and apply to varying extents to people from other countries. Perhaps the best use for physical appearancess is as an initial indicator, giving you a hint about which of the nine enneagram personality types a person belongs in.

Ones

Ones are not overly concerned with their image, but they usually have a neat and well-scrubbed look. Their fingernails are usually well cared for; however, some may bite them. Their hair may not be cut in the latest style, but it is clean and groomed.

Often Ones have a self-composed face and bright eyes. There can be a tightness around the mouth and jaws, and the lips may be thin. Because of the rigid way they hold their jaws, their voice can sound strained, as with Barbara Walters and Katharine Hepburn. They are usually thin, only seldom overweight.

Twos

Twos usually have a warm and attractive smile. Some have a problem with being overweight. They dress well and not flashily, generally wearing comfortable clothes of good quality but not always of the latest fashion. Normally they pay close attention when you talk to them.

Threes

Threes often look much younger than they are. Many have an all-American look and emanate a bright confidence. They can give you a big unwavering smile—but it's cooler than that of Twos.

Threes dress well. They dress for success and like to look sharp, without being either stylish or unstylish. However, their jewelry is likely to be in fashion, and their clothes appropriate for the occasion. Although they may have to work at keeping the pounds off, they are usually not overweight.

Fours

Fours often have a sad look, especially in their eyes, which may droop at the outer corners.

They dress anywhere from counterculture to the cutting edge of fashion, enjoying different looks and seeming to make each outfit work for them. Jewelry is popular with Fours, sometimes rather large pieces. They like to set off a solid color outfit with a belt, scarf, or beret in a dramatically different color. The key word is *drama*. They may even use a short dramatic pause before talking.

Fives

Fives often have a sparkle in their eyes. Sometimes a bit pudgy, they are seldom seriously overweight. They are not worried about how they look and couldn't care less about fashion. Although they may wear the same clothes for two days in a row, you will never see them wear anything soiled.

They do not have open and comfortable smiles, and they may have a weak chin, which male Fives are apt to conceal with a beard.

Sixes

Sixes sometimes have a protruding chin, and may be slightly shabby with badly kept fingernails. In dress, they go for comfort rather than chic, but make an exception when needed for the power look.

Many Sixes radiate a nervous energy. Their speech patterns can be halting.

Sevens

Sevens smile a lot. This is not a Three's radiant, confident smile nor a Two's warm smile—it may have a nervous quality to it, yet be a nice smile all the same. They can be teddybearish, but are usually not fat.

They dress fairly well and may have a sense of style. Some who are gourmets can be as selective and fastidious about clothes as about food. Sevens may wear a brightly colored scarf or sash for dramatic effect, but are not nearly as likely to do so as Fours.

Eights

Eights can be on the husky side, either with muscles from working out or with flab from overeating. On top of this, they are liable to wear massive jewelry. (For men, it's an open-neck shirt with heavy gold chains.) It's unnecessary to add that they are not overly concerned about their looks.

Eights are apt to strike people as being overbearing, perhaps even obstinate or angry.

Nines

Some Nines are overweight, some are thin. Often they have a heaviness about them, as if they found life too demanding and were drained of energy.

They like to wear jogging suits and other comfortable outfits, often well worn. At times they pull themselves together and dress up, but mostly they look slightly disheveled in their messy homes. Nines have an inert quality about them and usually impress others as being fairly relaxed and pleasant.

13

Enneagram Profiles

No approach to human personality, least of all that of the enneagram, enables us to attach labels to people with the expectation that they will henceforth behave according to rigid specifications. The enneagram, particularly, is not meant to be used as a branding iron, so that people can never erase the THREE or whatever stamped on their hide. Rather than limit or confine, the enneagram opens up psychic territory. It can be thought of as an investigative tool, something like Sherlock Holmes's magnifying glass or a radiotelescope aimed into deep space to receive tantalizing and sometimes mysterious signals.

With the caution that no system has yet succeeded in classifying humans into watertight compartments, and keeping in mind that people rarely behave exactly as we expect or think they should, nine short biographies are presented here, one for each of the nine enneagram personality types. The biographies may help the reader visualize what the personality types look like in flesh and blood.

Who are these people? Are they real or are they composite portraits, each one made up of the necessary ingredients of a particular enneagram personality type, like the recipe for a dish? They are all real. None are homogenized enneagram blueprints.

Being very real people, these individuals fit their enneagram personality type in different ways and to different degrees of completeness. But imperfect as they are, they are from real life—from what awaits you beyond the pages of this book. . . .

Ones

Bonnie. At twenty-two, Bonnie is unmarried and works as a ticket agent for a large airline. She is responsible and hardworking, trying to get every detail right in order to please people. Although she has high standards, she is not ambitious, being quite satisfied at her present job level. She wants to be financially comfortable but not necessarily make a lot of money.

She often complains about her luck with men, and how she always seems to get involved with the "wrong type." Even in a good relationship, she feels a lack of trust and deep intimacy.

Bonnie gets angry when she recalls how her mother treated her as a child. She believes her mother had an unconscious dislike of her ever since she was born, because she competed with her mother for her father's attention. He genuinely loved Bonnie, she feels, but owned a restaurant and seemed to be absent most of the time. In high school, she was moderately popular, yet underneath she felt shy.

Trying hard to be good and do the right thing, Bonnie leads a correct and very proper life. She pays a lot of attention to things of importance to her, such as her job and her membership in volunteer organizations. Sometimes she gets a bit overwhelmed with all the activities she takes on and in her efforts to balance all her commitments.

Bonnie is pleasant and well-mannered. At times, she likes to sit back and relax, joke and laugh.

Twos

Mary. Mary taught school for five years and then married a strong man who could take care of her. She picked a winner. He became a state judge, and she enjoys being the power behind the throne and supporting him. Now forty-six, she has four children, the eldest one in college.

Still in love with her husband after all these years, she keeps her children and his continued career success as her main goals in life. Mary quit her job when her first child was born and only went back to teaching when the kids got older. Now she works with handicapped children.

A good mother who spent a lot of time with her children, she had difficulty letting go of family control and allowing her children to develop into independent persons.

In her childhood, Mary was closer to her father than her mother, and was never very close to the only other child in the family, a brother. In high school, she was popular with everyone and had lots of boyfriends. Mary felt sad when she was alone; however, in public she was almost always happy. In spite of her popularity, she was not really a leader. On occasion, she could be aggressive—but always in a sweet way. After graduating from college, she taught at an elementary school and loved it.

Mary has never lost her sense of playfulness and is always willing to make pleasant small talk. While she likes to help others, she has no objection to being the center of attention herself.

Threes

Scott. Scott learned early in life that the way to get attention is to do something. His graduate degree—a master's in business administration—gave him a good start with the sales division of a prestigious manufacturing company. Push and hard work enabled him to climb the corporate ladder. Nearing retirement age (he's sixty-two), he plans to continue working and not let anyone put him out to pasture.

As a child, he was admired by his father for his ability to accomplish what he set out to do, but his father did not often express this admiration to his son. In high school, Scott took up bodybuilding and excelled at sports. Both there and later in college, he had good grades, good study habits, and fit in well socially with other students.

He married right after graduation, but it didn't work out. A few years later he married again, and this time found a more suitable partner. He has always put in long hours at work and never a great deal of time at home, but this has not been a problem in his second marriage because his wife has her own interests and they have no children.

Although Scott is a charming person, he can be abrupt. He always seems to be in a hurry to get on to the next thing on his list of priorities.

Fours

Patricia. Patricia had a series of short relationships before getting married and having two children. Her husband and she have had a stormy life together, with several separations and reconciliations. She is twenty-eight.

In her first jobs, Patricia had difficulties with supervisors who she felt did not understand her. Eventually she found a suitable job and is now a successful commercial artist, known for her sense of design.

As an unplanned baby, she was an inconvenience to her family, and she and her mother never got on. Her father died when she was six, and she still feels a special closeness to him. In high school, she was into alternate life-styles. She went on to art school, but dropped out after two years.

Patricia, while very close to her kids, feels it's important that her husband spend time with them too, so that she can have time to herself. She keeps her life interesting, creative, and dramatic. Involved in various political causes, she devotes most energy to Greenpeace. She also likes to read, go to movies, and travel.

Having stopped going to church while still young, Patricia has recently found God. She still feels she needs to do something unique and individual with her life.

Fives

Tim. Tim, now thirty, remembers that his mother had the ability to be both very present in his life and very absent from what was actually happening to him. His father spent much time on the road as a salesman and, when home, he often scared his son, sometimes with his coldness, other times with his anger.

In adolescence, Tim was very shy around girls. He was somewhat of a loner. In college, he gained self-confidence but never had more than a few friends. His grades were reasonably good, and he graduated with a math degree.

Tim works as a computer expert for U.S. Customs, and at his location he is the only one who can do what he does. But he never claims that he is indispensable; instead, he quietly and consistently turns in good work without supervision.

After a five-year engagement, he finally got married recently.

Tim likes to fantasize and daydream. He also reads a lot, and is a collector and tinkerer. One of his collections is of the different kinds of wood that grow in North America. He is happy with his life, and sees no reason why he will not continue to be, as long as he is comfortable and left alone when he desires.

Sixes

Frank. Frank is a thirty-three-year-old attorney with a successful practice in criminal law. He is happily married to a wife who stays at home to take care of their two kids in the style of the traditional American family. Frank is sweet to his daughter, tough on his son. His many friends find him somewhat aggressive and always antiauthority.

Frank's power struggles with authority began with his father, who was a strict disciplinarian. Frank was close to his mother. His troubles with authority continued through a rough adolescence, and he got into a fair amount of trouble. Then he straightened up and went to college—and continued to argue with his teachers. These days, Frank knows the limits of rebellion and how to play the game.

Although he is afraid of heights—to the point of getting nervous when standing on a ladder more than a few feet above the ground—he has taken pilot lessons and joined a club that is building its own airplane from precut aluminum parts. Frank has volunteered to be its test pilot.

Sevens

Kathy. Kathy wrote poetry and was the editor of her high school newspaper. After graduating from college, she became a professional journalist and continued to write poetry on the side.

The veteran of a number of relationships, at age thirty-four she is unmarried and unconcerned about it. She has a broad range of interests and is politically active. Her goal is to enjoy life and not suffer.

Because she was the first grandchild on both sides of her family, Kathy was treated like royalty—until her brother was born. She resented the way he diverted from her attention that had always been hers. Popular, she was a member of her high school swimming team.

Today Kathy mixes in many circles, and her separate sets of friends do not always get along together when they encounter each other through her. So far as Kathy is concerned, however, they are all her friends and fit just fine together.

Eights

John. Born into a poor family, John has eight sisters and brothers. He was the third child of a mild-tempered but overworked mother and an intimidating father. John was the family scapegoat, probably because he could not stand up to his father. When there was punishment to take, John was usually the one who took it.

He never had many friends and didn't much worry about it. After a year of college, he quit and became a police officer. He has had no regrets about that and, now twenty-four, he enjoys his career.

John is very intense and difficult to get to know, but once he is close to someone, he is a true friend. He is a champion of the underdog and a protector of the weak—and also a black belt in karate.

Married, he is fiercely loyal to his family and a tough but very loving father to his three children.

Nines

Sam. The youngest of three children, Sam was a bit lost in the shuffle. The members of his family were not particularly close to one another, but they all kept on pretty good terms.

He was shy as an adolescent and had acceptable but not spectacular grades. Sam had a fair number of friends and went on to the state university, where he earned a degree in political science.

Straight from college, Sam went into the family business, which consists of transforming industrial-size rolls of gift wrapping into domestic-use-size rolls and wholesaling them to local retail stores. On his twenty-ninth birthday, his father retired and he took over the business. He's a good administrator and easy to get along with.

Sam has a stable marriage and lives for his family and work. He enjoys spending time with his children. His goals in life are to be a good father, do a good job, and be—well, comfortable.

Part Four

Further into the
Enneagram

14

Stress Points
and Secure Points

In the enneagram star, each of the nine points is connected to two other points. This represents a relationship each of the nine personality types has with two others. The diagram on the next page shows the enneagram with arrows indicating directions of movement along these connecting lines. The personality type under stress tends to move in the direction of the arrow. For example, a One under stress tends to become a Four; that is, the person under stress is likely to drop many of his or her One characteristics and take up those of a Four.

In times of security, the personality type tends to move in the opposite direction to the arrow. Therefore a One would tend to behave like a Seven.

The personality type toward which you move under stress is called your stress point. The type you move toward when you feel secure is known as your secure point. For instance, a One's stress point is Four and secure point is Seven.

How can you know anyone's personality type if a person constantly bounces in and out of other personality types every time he or she feels stressed or secure? If we could transform ourselves easily from our normal personality type to another, things would indeed be very complex. But we

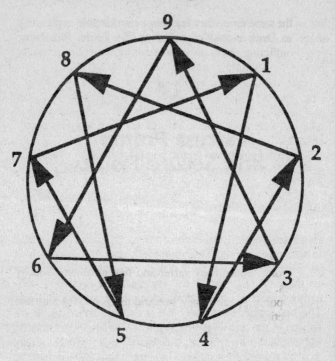

can't. As soon as a One under stress starts behaving like a Four, he or she begins to feel uncomfortable and retreats to being a One again. In other words, stress points and secure points are not very comfortable situations to be in, and we get back to our old familiar selves as quickly as we can.

The chief importance of stress points and secure points is that they represent potential for change. It is when we are veering toward one or the other that we are most likely to achieve personal growth. Being at the stress point is stressful, but dealing with this discomfort is what results in personal growth. For example, Ones under stress and veering toward Fours suffer and feel misunderstood by others.

But at the same time, they feel more comfortable expressing anger as Ones instead of suffering like Fours. Resolving such conflicting emotions in times of stress would certainly qualify as personal growth.

Healing takes place at the secure point, and this goes to the very foundation of personality. Although healing at a secure point sounds like a pleasant experience, in reality it is more likely to be an uncomfortable one. Change is nearly always difficult.

The stress points and secure points for the nine enneagram personality types are described in the following paragraphs, with some comments on each.

Ones

Stress point: Four. They suffer and feel misunderstood by others.
Secure point: Seven. They become more playful and less perfectionist.

Twos

Stress point: Eight. They get angry.
Secure point: Four. They are more able to show sadness and to cry.

Threes

Stress point: Nine. They become out of touch with their feelings and operate more mechanically.
Secure point: Six. They are more cooperative and less concerned with status.

Fours

Stress point: Two. They please, charm, and flatter others.
Secure point: One. They become more neat and
   perfectionist.

Fives

Stress point: Seven. They plan and daydream instead of
   taking action.
Secure point: Eight. They are more assertive and involved
   with others.

Sixes

Stress point: Three. They become anxious and take action
   defensively.
Secure point: Nine. They relax, are more self-assured, and
   make decisions.

Sevens

Stress point: One. They become judgmental, pessimistic,
   and perfectionist.
Secure point: Five. They move into work and production,
   and spend less time daydreaming.

Eights

Stress point: Five. They run away and hide.
Secure point: Two. They are more playful, joyful, and interested in pleasing people.

Nines

Stress point: Six. They become afraid, self-doubting, and indecisive.
Secure point: Three. They become more energetic, involved in life, and successful.

15

Wings

Each personality type has two wings. These are the numbers on either side of it on the enneagram. Thus the wings of personality type Two are One and Three, and those of One are Nine and Two. Most people have one dominant wing. To put all that in plain words, one of the two personality types adjoining yours has an effect on you. But which one?

To find your dominant wing, you must of course have found your personality type. Take the True or False Test for each of the personality types on either side of yours. The wing with the highest score is your dominant wing.

Your dominant wing can affect your personality in many ways, particularly in the area of personal growth. The possible wings for each enneagram personality type are given below, with observations about their effects.

Ones

Leaning toward Nine: They are less self-concerned, less vain, and more easygoing, but smile less readily.

Leaning toward Two: They are more concerned with how they look and with getting attention from others. They are more dramatic in their presentation, more sensitive to others, and more proud.

Twos

Leaning toward One: They are lazier, have less energy, and are more concerned with things being right.

Leaning toward Three: They have a harder edge and are more aggressive, but this can be aggressive seduction.

Threes

Leaning toward Two: They take on the feelings of others.

Leaning toward Four: They dramatize their own feelings.

Fours

Leaning toward Three: They are more aggressive and out in the world getting things accomplished, but they tend to sabotage success in their private life.

Leaning toward Five: They are more withdrawn and isolated.

Fives

Leaning toward Four: They are more into their feelings, more artistic, and more melancholic.

Leaning toward Six: They operate intellectually, disconnected from their own feelings and less connected emotionally with others.

Sixes

Leaning toward Five: They are softer, quieter, and more withdrawn.

Leaning toward Seven: They are more aggressive, out there dealing with the world, and optimistic.

Sevens

Leaning toward Six: They are more unsure of themselves, have a subtle nervous energy, and are hesitant of action.

Leaning toward Eight: They have more a sense of their own power, are tougher and more aggressive.

Eights

Leaning toward Seven: They are more intellectual, idealistic, and into planning.

Leaning toward Nine: They are more pragmatic and act more from the gut than the head.

Nines

Leaning toward Eight: They dress sloppier and become more overtly angry.

Leaning toward One: They are more in control of themselves and their environment. They have more of a sense of how things should be. Their anger is more repressed.

16

Identification Difficulties

The vast majority of people who take the tests given in this book quickly discover their enneagram personality type—and agree with the outcome. As with any personality test, a small percentage will have difficulty deciding upon or agreeing with the results. There are four main reasons for this.

1. Those who have carried out extensive psychological self-examination can be misidentified according to enneagram personality type. Such people, in taking the tests, should try to respond as they would have before their psychological self-examination.

2. An especially strong dominant wing (see Chapter 15, "Wings") can mask the basic characteristics of an individual's personality type.

3. Some people have difficulty being introspective enough to answer the test questions correctly.

4. The tests were designed for normal, emotionally healthy people. People undergoing emotional disturbance or psychological trauma can be misidentified as to personality type.

17

How Good Are You at Using the Enneagram?

The purpose of this book is to help you find your enneagram personality type. In doing this, the book serves only as a very brief introduction to enneagram studies in general. So, be warned. Even after you have mastered everything in this book, you are not an enneagram expert!

But it's important to know how good you are right now at using the enneagram—the more accurate you can prove yourself to be, the more you can depend on your results. After all, you are making decisions about yourself and other people. Thus, being accurate with the enneagram can have important consequences in your life.

The best way to test your accuracy in using the enneagram is to pick a personality type other than your own (or one you are familiar with) and put it to the True or False Test. This time, for each of the fifty statements, score one point for each correct answer and zero for incorrect and those you can't answer. Clearly, the higher your score, the better you understand this personality type. The chart following ranks your accuracy in using the enneagram.

Score	Rank
Below 40	Beginner
40 to 45	Good
45 to 48	Excellent
Over 48	Superior

If your score was very low (or very high), you may have picked on a personality type particularly hard (or easy) for you to understand. Doing the same test with other personality types will give you a more representative average of your performing accuracy with the enneagram.

18

Childhood Influences

Nature or nurture? It has been argued for decades whether children are born with a personality—nature—or learn a personality from their environment—nurture. Most authorities today agree that *both* processes take place, that both our genetic heritage and our environment as very young children help shape our personality. In some cases, one may clearly predominate over the other.

Since no one has seriously suggested that we inherit our enneagram personality type from our parents through genes, it is reasonable to assume that we pick it up in our early environment. But this does not mean that our parents do not influence our enneagram personality type. They do, and very strongly, by contributing to what we feel when we think about ourselves as individuals.

Early in life, children develop a special sense of self. One factor that is a great influence on children's personality is where they get their sense of self from. Usually this is from a parent or substitute parent, such as a grandparent or older relative living with the family. Children can get their special sense of self from a parent even if little time is spent with this parent, or even if this is not the favorite parent.

The following are the most clear-cut general enneagram relations between parents (or substitute parents) and offspring:

Very Influential Parent	_Offspring's Most Likely Type_
Father	Two, Three, or Four
Mother	Five, Six, or Seven
Father usually	One
Mother usually	Eight
Either parent	Nine

Children attempt to resolve their fundamental needs from their environment. In their attempts to make sense of this environment, they begin to function as one of the nine enneagram personality types. The childhood scenarios that follow may seem somewhat negative, but it is children's preoccupation with these perceived negatives that influences their development into particular enneagram personality types. The circumstances and details can be expected to vary widely with individuals. This childhood information was developed by Thomas Mellin, an internationally known enneagram teacher.

Ones

Ones have usually gotten their special sense of self from their father. They have often felt emotionally abandoned by both parents at an early age. The One child need not have been close to the father to be deeply influenced by him. The mother may have been ill or preoccupied by divorce or emotional issues, or some other circumstances may have been responsible for the lack of emotional closeness between her and the child.

Sometimes the One child has been required to assume grown-up responsibilities and care for younger members of the family. Such children perceive the expectation that they must be well behaved, follow rules, constantly improve, and not get angry. They tend to bond to rules and to have a difficult time knowing what real emotional connectedness is.

Both One and Nine children tend to have been ignored, but Ones also may have been much more criticized, or in extreme cases even abused, for failing to live up to their parents' standards.

Twos

Twos have a very special tie with their father, especially females who have been daddy's little girl. Twos have needed their father's attention and tried to be what he wanted them to be. In cases where he was distant, the Two child tried even harder. As children, Twos have probably felt emotionally insecure about their mother. When feeling ill or sad, they have tried to look all right in order to please their father. They have perceived that people like them if they are loving, pleasantly spoken, and nicely behaved.

Threes

Threes are less strongly influenced by their father than Twos. Although Threes as children have tried to get their father's attention by what they could do, they never seem to have fully succeeded in getting it, with the result that they have slipped into an endless attention-seeking performance role. As children, Threes do not get their special sense of self from consciousness of their individuality but from what they can accomplish or achieve.

Fours

Besides getting their special sense of self from their father, Fours often experience an emotional abandonment, or in extreme cases a physical abandonment, by their mother. This increases the closeness to the father and perhaps contributes to its frequently antagonistic, distorted, or negative quality that results in an unhappy childhood. As children, Fours retreat inward in emotions and fantasies.

Fives

Getting their special sense of self from their mother, Fives as children tend to perceive their father as scary and distant. They have often been relatively ignored by both parents—perhaps even told to stay out of the way by their mother. In early childhood, they have had a powerful experience of unfulfilled need, for example, not enough milk at the breast, not enough time with parents, or not enough holding and affection. The children have wanted to be angry about this but have found anger to be too frightening an emotion.

Sixes

The mother is the most influential parent for Sixes. Unlike One children, who have been brought up with clear rules, Six children have been raised with ambiguous rules. Their parents have laid down inconsistent rules, with limits not clearly defined. The children have come to feel that rules are a mine field in which it is easy to break a rule you didn't even know existed—with dire consequences. One wrong step can be disastrous, and you never know which step that will be. As children, Sixes are closer to the mother and may be afraid of the father.

Sevens

The mother gives the special sense of self to Sevens. They have probably been mother's special person, but at some early stage of their life, this special connection has been lost. This may have been caused by the birth of another child or the return of the mother to work. The perceived loss has left a yearning to restore the original close tie to the mother, and the child may have tried to reestablish such a connection with another woman, such as a grandmother or aunt. Such children, feeling their loss, tend to direct their anger toward their father rather than their mother.

Before the withdrawal of the mother's attention, the child may have been enrolled in "saving" the mother or making her life complete. The child keeps trying to be pleasant to the mother in order to get back that special tie, but underneath has a sense of emotional abandonment. The child does not want to rely on pleasantness alone and wants a backup plan. Sevens usually have pleasant childhood memories, of their mother in particular.

Eights

Usually Eights get their special sense of self from their mother. They have often come from families that attempted to overdominate their life, either physically or emotionally. They have challenged this domination, even though they had to fight adults or older children representing overwhelming odds. Eights may deny they had a bad childhood but admit they had to struggle against powerful people. Some Eights have been emotionally abandoned children.

Nines

Either the father or mother gives the sense of self to Nines. As children, Nines perceive themselves as not loved enough or listened to by their parents, and possibly even see themselves as emotionally abandoned. They have often been the firstborn who got lost as the other children come along. They may have had to take care of the other children, like a third parent, and lacked enough personal attention for themselves. Generally they have not been as criticized or controlled as One children, but are victims of benign neglect. Sometimes Nines have been the youngest child who got treated mechanically and ignored. Nines tend to believe they have taken a back seat to other members of the family. They have probably not been given a strong sense of themselves as children, and typically their shows of anger never produced desired results.

Before the withdrawal of the mother's attention, the child
may have been enrolled in "saving." The mother or making
to the that mother's "the smile has learned to be pleasant.

19

Expanding the Enneagram into Subtypes

Although the nine personality types represented by the
points of the enneagram star are sufficient in themselves to
gain a deep insight into human personality, some people
find it useful to expand the enneagram threefold, from nine
types into twenty-seven subtypes. This is done by subdi-
viding each personality type into social, self-preservation,
and individual subtypes. This is illustrated in the figure on
the next page, where

I = individual subtype
P = self-preservation subtype
S = social subtype

Social Subtype

People who belong to a social subtype, as the name implies,
tend to be open with everyone on a more or less equal level.
Emotionally, they are the most mellow of the three subtypes.
Words of special meaning to members of a social subtype
include *duty*, *dishonor*, *friendship*, *prestige*, *commitment*,
participation, and *status*.

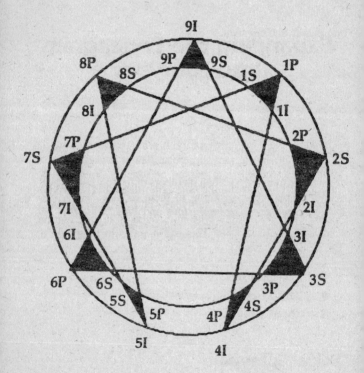

Self-preservation Subtype

A sparseness or lack of quality in personal relationships is typical of people who belong in a self-preservation subtype. When pushed by others, they more quickly become self-defensive. Words of special significance to them include *security*, *defender*, *danger*, *hunger*, *alliance*, *residence*, *homeland*, and *survival*.

Individual Subtype

People who belong to an individual subtype have a higher energy than people who belong to the other two subtypes. There is a brightness to their eyes, and they are concerned with relating to people one on one. They want to be in touch with their senses, and also aware of their destiny. However, they can be more erratic than members of the other subtypes. Words of particular meaning to them include *beauty*, *intensity*, *confidence*, *strength*, *love* and *hate*, *sexuality*, *seduction*, *primary relationship*, and *jealousy*.

20

Where to Find More Information

It has already been said that this book represents only a small portion of a vast trove of knowledge built up over the centuries in an ancient and once-secret system. Throughout most of its history, knowledge of the enneagram has been passed from generation to generation through oral teaching. Even today, many teachers believe that no book, tape, or test can be as precise as the feedback from a teacher who truly understands the enneagram system.

Seminars are an excellent way to learn more about the enneagram, and they are available in many cities all over America. The following seminar leaders are recommended. They hold classes in many cities in addition to their hometowns. Write or phone for the latest schedules.

Seminar Leaders

Ed Hackerson
115 Humboldt, San Rafael, CA 94903
(916) 272–0971

Enneagram Personality Types (Don Riso)
222 Riverside Drive, Suite 10E, New York, NY 10025
(212) 932–3306

Maria Beesing and Patrick O'Leary
P.O. Box 360427, Cleveland, OH 44136
(216) 243–8870

John Burchill and Barbara Metz
20 Glen Street, Dover MA 02030–0370
(617) 785–0124

Books

Maria Beesing, Robert Nogosek, and Patrick O'Leary, *The Enneagram*, Denville, NJ: Dimension Books, 1984

Kathleen Hurley and Theodore Dobson, *What's My Type?*, San Francisco: Harper, 1991

Claudio Naranjo, *Ennea-type Structures*, Nevada City, CA: Gateways/IDHHB, 1990

Helen Palmer, *The Enneagram*, San Francisco: Harper, 1988

Don Riso, *Personality Types*, Boston: Houghton Mifflin, 1987

Don Riso, *Understanding the Enneagram*, Boston: Houghton Mifflin, 1990

Richard Rohr and Andreas Ebert, *Discovering the Enneagram*, New York: Crossroad, 1990

Bernard Tickerhoof, *Conversion & the Enneagram*, Denville, NJ: Dimension Books, 1991

Additional
Score Sheets

Quick Test Score Sheet

1. 1   2   3   4   5   6   7   8   9   10
least agreement   most agreement

2. 1   2   3   4   5   6   7   8   9   10
least agreement   most agreement

3. 1   2   3   4   5   6   7   8   9   10
least agreement   most agreement

4. 1   2   3   4   5   6   7   8   9   10
least agreement   most agreement

5. 1   2   3   4   5   6   7   8   9   10
least agreement   most agreement

6. 1   2   3   4   5   6   7   8   9   10
least agreement   most agreement

7. 1   2   3   4   5   6   7   8   9   10
least agreement   most agreement

8. 1   2   3   4   5   6   7   8   9   10
least agreement   most agreement

9. 1   2   3   4   5   6   7   8   9   10
least agreement   most agreement

10. 1   2   3   4   5   6   7   8   9   10
least agreement   most agreement

11. 1   2   3   4   5   6   7   8   9   10
least agreement   most agreement

12. 1   2   3   4   5   6   7   8   9   10
least agreement   most agreement

13. 1   2   3   4   5   6   7   8   9   10
least agreement   most agreement

14. 1   2   3   4   5   6   7   8   9   10
least agreement   most agreement

15. 1   2   3   4   5   6   7   8   9   10
least agreement   most agreement

16. 1   2   3   4   5   6   7   8   9   10
least agreement   most agreement

17. 1   2   3   4   5   6   7   8   9   10
least agreement   most agreement

18. 1   2   3   4   5   6   7   8   9   10
least agreement   most agreement

Quick Test Score Sheet (cont.)

19. 1   2   3   4   5   6   7   8   9   10
least agreement   most agreement

20. 1   2   3   4   5   6   7   8   9   10
least agreement   most agreement

21. 1   2   3   4   5   6   7   8   9   10
least agreement   most agreement

22. 1   2   3   4   5   6   7   8   9   10
least agreement   most agreement

23. 1   2   3   4   5   6   7   8   9   10
least agreement   most agreement

24. 1   2   3   4   5   6   7   8   9   10
least agreement   most agreement

25. 1   2   3   4   5   6   7   8   9   10
least agreement   most agreement

26. 1   2   3   4   5   6   7   8   9   10
least agreement   most agreement

27. 1   2   3   4   5   6   7   8   9   10
least agreement   most agreement

Transfer your scores from the score sheet to the following boxes. Total the scores in each of the nine boxes.

Quick Test Boxes

1._____
2._____
3._____
Total _____
Personality
Type One

4._____
5._____
6._____
Total _____
Personality
Type Two

7._____
8._____
9._____
Total _____
Personality
Type Three

10._____
11._____
12._____
Total _____
Personality
Type Four

13._____
14._____
15._____
Total _____
Personality
Type Five

16._____
17._____
18._____
Total _____
Personality
Type Six

19._____
20._____
21._____
Total _____
Personality
Type Seven

22._____
23._____
24._____
Total _____
Personality
Type Eight

25._____
26._____
27._____
Total _____
Personality
Type Nine

True or False Score Sheet

Ones	Twos	Threes	Fours	Fives	Sixes	Sevens	Eights	Nines
1.___	1.___	1.___	1.___	1.___	1.___	1.___	1.___	1.___
2.___	2.___	2.___	2.___	2.___	2.___	2.___	2.___	2.___
3.___	3.___	3.___	3.___	3.___	3.___	3.___	3.___	3.___
4.___	4.___	4.___	4.___	4.___	4.___	4.___	4.___	4.___
5.___	5.___	5.___	5.___	5.___	5.___	5.___	5.___	5.___
6.___	6.___	6.___	6.___	6.___	6.___	6.___	6.___	6.___
7.___	7.___	7.___	7.___	7.___	7.___	7.___	7.___	7.___
8.___	8.___	8.___	8.___	8.___	8.___	8.___	8.___	8.___
9.___	9.___	9.___	9.___	9.___	9.___	9.___	9.___	9.___
10.___	10.___	10.___	10.___	10.___	10.___	10.___	10.___	10.___
11.___	11.___	11.___	11.___	11.___	11.___	11.___	11.___	11.___
12.___	12.___	12.___	12.___	12.___	12.___	12.___	12.___	12.___
13.___	13.___	13.___	13.___	13.___	13.___	13.___	13.___	13.___
14.___	14.___	14.___	14.___	14.___	14.___	14.___	14.___	14.___
15.___	15.___	15.___	15.___	15.___	15.___	15.___	15.___	15.___
16.___	16.___	16.___	16.___	16.___	16.___	16.___	16.___	16.___
17.___	17.___	17.___	17.___	17.___	17.___	17.___	17.___	17.___
18.___	18.___	18.___	18.___	18.___	18.___	18.___	18.___	18.___
19.___	19.___	19.___	19.___	19.___	19.___	19.___	19.___	19.___
20.___	20.___	20.___	20.___	20.___	20.___	20.___	20.___	20.___
21.___	21.___	21.___	21.___	21.___	21.___	21.___	21.___	21.___
22.___	22.___	22.___	22.___	22.___	22.___	22.___	22.___	22.___
23.___	23.___	23.___	23.___	23.___	23.___	23.___	23.___	23.___
24.___	24.___	24.___	24.___	24.___	24.___	24.___	24.___	24.___
25.___	25.___	25.___	25.___	25.___	25.___	25.___	25.___	25.___
26.___	26.___	26.___	26.___	26.___	26.___	26.___	26.___	26.___
27.___	27.___	27.___	27.___	27.___	27.___	27.___	27.___	27.___
28.___	28.___	28.___	28.___	28.___	28.___	28.___	28.___	28.___
29.___	29.___	29.___	29.___	29.___	29.___	29.___	29.___	29.___
30.___	30.___	30.___	30.___	30.___	30.___	30.___	30.___	30.___
31.___	31.___	31.___	31.___	31.___	31.___	31.___	31.___	31.___
32.___	32.___	32.___	32.___	32.___	32.___	32.___	32.___	32.___
33.___	33.___	33.___	33.___	33.___	33.___	33.___	33.___	33.___
34.___	34.___	34.___	34.___	34.___	34.___	34.___	34.___	34.___
35.___	35.___	35.___	35.___	35.___	35.___	35.___	35.___	35.___
36.___	36.___	36.___	36.___	36.___	36.___	36.___	36.___	36.___
37.___	37.___	37.___	37.___	37.___	37.___	37.___	37.___	37.___
38.___	38.___	38.___	38.___	38.___	38.___	38.___	38.___	38.___
39.___	39.___	39.___	39.___	39.___	39.___	39.___	39.___	39.___
40.___	40.___	40.___	40.___	40.___	40.___	40.___	40.___	40.___
41.___	41.___	41.___	41.___	41.___	41.___	41.___	41.___	41.___
42.___	42.___	42.___	42.___	42.___	42.___	42.___	42.___	42.___
43.___	43.___	43.___	43.___	43.___	43.___	43.___	43.___	43.___
44.___	44.___	44.___	44.___	44.___	44.___	44.___	44.___	44.___
45.___	45.___	45.___	45.___	45.___	45.___	45.___	45.___	45.___
46.___	46.___	46.___	46.___	46.___	46.___	46.___	46.___	46.___
47.___	47.___	47.___	47.___	47.___	47.___	47.___	47.___	47.___
48.___	48.___	48.___	48.___	48.___	48.___	48.___	48.___	48.___
49.___	49.___	49.___	49.___	49.___	49.___	49.___	49.___	49.___
50.___	50.___	50.___	50.___	50.___	50.___	50.___	50.___	50.___
SCORE	SCORE	SCORE	SCORE	SCORE	SCORE	SCORE	SCORE	SCORE

Quick Test Score Sheet

1. 1   2   3   4   5   6   7   8   9   10
least agreement   most agreement

2. 1   2   3   4   5   6   7   8   9   10
least agreement   most agreement

3. 1   2   3   4   5   6   7   8   9   10
least agreement   most agreement

4. 1   2   3   4   5   6   7   8   9   10
least agreement   most agreement

5. 1   2   3   4   5   6   7   8   9   10
least agreement   most agreement

6. 1   2   3   4   5   6   7   8   9   10
least agreement   most agreement

7. 1   2   3   4   5   6   7   8   9   10
least agreement   most agreement

8. 1   2   3   4   5   6   7   8   9   10
least agreement   most agreement

9. 1   2   3   4   5   6   7   8   9   10
least agreement   most agreement

10. 1   2   3   4   5   6   7   8   9   10
least agreement   most agreement

11. 1   2   3   4   5   6   7   8   9   10
least agreement   most agreement

12. 1   2   3   4   5   6   7   8   9   10
least agreement   most agreement

13. 1   2   3   4   5   6   7   8   9   10
least agreement   most agreement

14. 1   2   3   4   5   6   7   8   9   10
least agreement   most agreement

15. 1   2   3   4   5   6   7   8   9   10
least agreement   most agreement

16. 1   2   3   4   5   6   7   8   9   10
least agreement   most agreement

17. 1   2   3   4   5   6   7   8   9   10
least agreement   most agreement

18. 1   2   3   4   5   6   7   8   9   10
least agreement   most agreement

Quick Test Score Sheet (cont.)

19. 1   2   3   4   5   6   7   8   9   10
    least agreement   most agreement

20. 1   2   3   4   5   6   7   8   9   10
    least agreement   most agreement

21. 1   2   3   4   5   6   7   8   9   10
    least agreement   most agreement

22. 1   2   3   4   5   6   7   8   9   10
    least agreement   most agreement

23. 1   2   3   4   5   6   7   8   9   10
    least agreement   most agreement

24. 1   2   3   4   5   6   7   8   9   10
    least agreement   most agreement

25. 1   2   3   4   5   6   7   8   9   10
    least agreement   most agreement

26. 1   2   3   4   5   6   7   8   9   10
    least agreement   most agreement

27. 1   2   3   4   5   6   7   8   9   10
    least agreement   most agreement

Transfer your scores from the score sheet to the following boxes. Total the scores in each of the nine boxes.

Quick Test Boxes

| 1._____ |
| 2._____ |
| 3._____ |
| Total _____ |
| Personality |
| Type One |

| 4._____ |
| 5._____ |
| 6._____ |
| Total _____ |
| Personality |
| Type Two |

| 7._____ |
| 8._____ |
| 9._____ |
| Total _____ |
| Personality |
| Type Three |

| 10._____ |
| 11._____ |
| 12._____ |
| Total _____ |
| Personality |
| Type Four |

| 13._____ |
| 14._____ |
| 15._____ |
| Total _____ |
| Personality |
| Type Five |

| 16._____ |
| 17._____ |
| 18._____ |
| Total _____ |
| Personality |
| Type Six |

| 19._____ |
| 20._____ |
| 21._____ |
| Total _____ |
| Personality |
| Type Seven |

| 22._____ |
| 23._____ |
| 24._____ |
| Total _____ |
| Personality |
| Type Eight |

| 25._____ |
| 26._____ |
| 27._____ |
| Total _____ |
| Personality |
| Type Nine |

True or False Score Sheet

Ones	Twos	Threes	Fours	Fives	Sixes	Sevens	Eights	Nines
1.___	1.___	1.___	1.___	1.___	1.___	1.___	1.___	1.___
2.___	2.___	2.___	2.___	2.___	2.___	2.___	2.___	2.___
3.___	3.___	3.___	3.___	3.___	3.___	3.___	3.___	3.___
4.___	4.___	4.___	4.___	4.___	4.___	4.___	4.___	4.___
5.___	5.___	5.___	5.___	5.___	5.___	5.___	5.___	5.___
6.___	6.___	6.___	6.___	6.___	6.___	6.___	6.___	6.___
7.___	7.___	7.___	7.___	7.___	7.___	7.___	7.___	8.___
8.___	8.___	8.___	8.___	8.___	8.___	8.___	8.___	8.___
9.___	9.___	9.___	9.___	9.___	9.___	9.___	9.___	9.___
10.___	10.___	10.___	10.___	10.___	10.___	10.___	10.___	10.___
11.___	11.___	11.___	11.___	11.___	11.___	11.___	11.___	11.___
12.___	12.___	12.___	12.___	12.___	12.___	12.___	12.___	12.___
13.___	13.___	13.___	13.___	13.___	13.___	13.___	13.___	13.___
14.___	14.___	14.___	14.___	14.___	14.___	14.___	14.___	14.___
15.___	15.___	15.___	15.___	15.___	15.___	15.___	15.___	15.___
16.___	16.___	16.___	16.___	16.___	16.___	16.___	16.___	16.___
17.___	17.___	17.___	17.___	17.___	17.___	17.___	17.___	17.___
18.___	18.___	18.___	18.___	18.___	18.___	18.___	18.___	18.___
19.___	19.___	19.___	19.___	19.___	19.___	19.___	19.___	19.___
20.___	20.___	20.___	20.___	20.___	20.___	20.___	20.___	20.___
21.___	21.___	21.___	21.___	21.___	21.___	21.___	21.___	21.___
22.___	22.___	22.___	22.___	22.___	22.___	22.___	22.___	22.___
23.___	23.___	23.___	23.___	23.___	23.___	23.___	23.___	23.___
24.___	24.___	24.___	24.___	24.___	24.___	24.___	24.___	24.___
25.___	25.___	25.___	25.___	25.___	25.___	25.___	25.___	25.___
26.___	26.___	26.___	26.___	26.___	26.___	26.___	26.___	26.___
27.___	27.___	27.___	27.___	27.___	27.___	27.___	27.___	27.___
28.___	28.___	28.___	28.___	28.___	28.___	28.___	28.___	28.___
29.___	29.___	29.___	29.___	29.___	29.___	29.___	29.___	29.___
30.___	30.___	30.___	30.___	30.___	30.___	30.___	30.___	30.___
31.___	31.___	31.___	31.___	31.___	31.___	31.___	31.___	31.___
32.___	32.___	32.___	32.___	32.___	32.___	32.___	32.___	32.___
33.___	33.___	33.___	33.___	33.___	33.___	33.___	33.___	33.___
34.___	34.___	34.___	34.___	34.___	34.___	34.___	34.___	34.___
35.___	35.___	35.___	35.___	35.___	35.___	35.___	35.___	35.___
36.___	36.___	36.___	36.___	36.___	36.___	36.___	36.___	36.___
37.___	37.___	37.___	37.___	37.___	37.___	37.___	37.___	37.___
38.___	38.___	38.___	38.___	38.___	38.___	38.___	38.___	38.___
39.___	39.___	39.___	39.___	39.___	39.___	39.___	39.___	39.___
40.___	40.___	40.___	40.___	40.___	40.___	40.___	40.___	40.___
41.___	41.___	41.___	41.___	41.___	41.___	41.___	41.___	41.___
42.___	42.___	42.___	42.___	42.___	42.___	42.___	42.___	42.___
43.___	43.___	43.___	43.___	43.___	43.___	43.___	43.___	43.___
44.___	44.___	44.___	44.___	44.___	44.___	44.___	44.___	44.___
45.___	45.___	45.___	45.___	45.___	45.___	45.___	45.___	45.___
46.___	46.___	46.___	46.___	46.___	46.___	46.___	46.___	46.___
47.___	47.___	47.___	47.___	47.___	47.___	47.___	47.___	47.___
48.___	48.___	48.___	48.___	48.___	48.___	48.___	48.___	48.___
49.___	49.___	49.___	49.___	49.___	49.___	49.___	49.___	49.___
50.___	50.___	50.___	50.___	50.___	50.___	50.___	50.___	50.___
SCORE	SCORE	SCORE	SCORE	SCORE	SCORE	SCORE	SCORE	SCORE

Quick Test Score Sheet

1. 1   2   3   4   5   6   7   8   9   10
least agreement   most agreement

2. 1   2   3   4   5   6   7   8   9   10
least agreement   most agreement

3. 1   2   3   4   5   6   7   8   9   10
least agreement   most agreement

4. 1   2   3   4   5   6   7   8   9   10
least agreement   most agreement

5. 1   2   3   4   5   6   7   8   9   10
least agreement   most agreement

6. 1   2   3   4   5   6   7   8   9   10
least agreement   most agreement

7. 1   2   3   4   5   6   7   8   9   10
least agreement   most agreement

8. 1   2   3   4   5   6   7   8   9   10
least agreement   most agreement

9. 1   2   3   4   5   6   7   8   9   10
least agreement   most agreement

10. 1   2   3   4   5   6   7   8   9   10
least agreement   most agreement

11. 1   2   3   4   5   6   7   8   9   10
least agreement   most agreement

12. 1   2   3   4   5   6   7   8   9   10
least agreement   most agreement

13. 1   2   3   4   5   6   7   8   9   10
least agreement   most agreement

14. 1   2   3   4   5   6   7   8   9   10
least agreement   most agreement

15. 1   2   3   4   5   6   7   8   9   10
least agreement   most agreement

16. 1   2   3   4   5   6   7   8   9   10
least agreement   most agreement

17. 1   2   3   4   5   6   7   8   9   10
least agreement   most agreement

18. 1   2   3   4   5   6   7   8   9   10
least agreement   most agreement

Quick Test Score Sheet (cont.)

19. 1   2   3   4   5   6   7   8   9   10
    least agreement   most agreement

20. 1   2   3   4   5   6   7   8   9   10
    least agreement   most agreement

21. 1   2   3   4   5   6   7   8   9   10
    least agreement   most agreement

22. 1   2   3   4   5   6   7   8   9   10
    least agreement   most agreement

23. 1   2   3   4   5   6   7   8   9   10
    least agreement   most agreement

24. 1   2   3   4   5   6   7   8   9   10
    least agreement   most agreement

25. 1   2   3   4   5   6   7   8   9   10
    least agreement   most agreement

26. 1   2   3   4   5   6   7   8   9   10
    least agreement   most agreement

27. 1   2   3   4   5   6   7   8   9   10
    least agreement   most agreement

Transfer your scores from the score sheet to the following boxes. Total the scores in each of the nine boxes.

Quick Test Boxes

1._____
2._____
3._____
Total _____
Personality
Type One

4._____
5._____
6._____
Total _____
Personality
Type Two

7._____
8._____
9._____
Total _____
Personality
Type Three

10._____
11._____
12._____
Total _____
Personality
Type Four

13._____
14._____
15._____
Total _____
Personality
Type Five

16._____
17._____
18._____
Total _____
Personality
Type Six

19._____
20._____
21._____
Total _____
Personality
Type Seven

22._____
23._____
24._____
Total _____
Personality
Type Eight

25._____
26._____
27._____
Total _____
Personality
Type Nine

True or False Score Sheet

Ones	Twos	Threes	Fours	Fives	Sixes	Sevens	Eights	Nines
1.	1.	1.	1.	1.	1.	1.	1.	1.
2.	2.	2.	2.	2.	2.	2.	2.	2.
3.	3.	3.	3.	3.	3.	3.	3.	3.
4.	4.	4.	4.	4.	4.	4.	4.	4.
5.	5.	5.	5.	5.	5.	5.	5.	5.
6.	6.	6.	6.	6.	6.	6.	6.	6.
7.	7.	7.	7.	7.	7.	7.	7.	8.
8.	8.	8.	8.	8.	8.	8.	8.	8.
9.	9.	9.	9.	9.	9.	9.	9.	9.
10.	10.	10.	10.	10.	10.	10.	10.	10.
11.	11.	11.	11.	11.	11.	11.	11.	11.
12.	12.	12.	12.	12.	12.	12.	12.	12.
13.	13.	13.	13.	13.	13.	13.	13.	13.
14.	14.	14.	14.	14.	14.	14.	14.	14.
15.	15.	15.	15.	15.	15.	15.	15.	15.
16.	16.	16.	16.	16.	16.	16.	16.	16.
17.	17.	17.	17.	17.	17.	17.	17.	17.
18.	18.	18.	18.	18.	18.	18.	18.	18.
19.	19.	19.	19.	19.	19.	19.	19.	19.
20.	20.	20.	20.	20.	20.	20.	20.	20.
21.	21.	21.	21.	21.	21.	21.	21.	21.
22.	22.	22.	22.	22.	22.	22.	22.	22.
23.	23.	23.	23.	23.	23.	23.	23.	23.
24.	24.	24.	24.	24.	24.	24.	24.	24.
25.	25.	25.	25.	25.	25.	25.	25.	25.
26.	26.	26.	26.	26.	26.	26.	26.	26.
27.	27.	27.	27.	27.	27.	27.	27.	27.
28.	28.	28.	28.	28.	28.	28.	28.	28.
29.	29.	29.	29.	29.	29.	29.	29.	29.
30.	30.	30.	30.	30.	30.	30.	30.	30.
31.	31.	31.	31.	31.	31.	31.	31.	31.
32.	32.	32.	32.	32.	32.	32.	32.	32.
33.	33.	33.	33.	33.	33.	33.	33.	33.
34.	34.	34.	34.	34.	34.	34.	34.	34.
35.	35.	35.	35.	35.	35.	35.	35.	35.
36.	36.	36.	36.	36.	36.	36.	36.	36.
37.	37.	37.	37.	37.	37.	37.	37.	37.
38.	38.	38.	38.	38.	38.	38.	38.	38.
39.	39.	39.	39.	39.	39.	39.	39.	39.
40.	40.	40.	40.	40.	40.	40.	40.	40.
41.	41.	41.	41.	41.	41.	41.	41.	41.
42.	42.	42.	42.	42.	42.	42.	42.	42.
43.	43.	43.	43.	43.	43.	43.	43.	43.
44.	44.	44.	44.	44.	44.	44.	44.	44.
45.	45.	45.	45.	45.	45.	45.	45.	45.
46.	46.	46.	46.	46.	46.	46.	46.	46.
47.	47.	47.	47.	47.	47.	47.	47.	47.
48.	48.	48.	48.	48.	48.	48.	48.	48.
49.	49.	49.	49.	49.	49.	49.	49.	49.
50.	50.	50.	50.	50.	50.	50.	50.	50.

| SCORE | SCORE | SCORE | SCORE | SCORE | SCORE | SCORE | SCORE | SCORE |

Quick Test Score Sheet

1. 1   2   3   4   5   6   7   8   9   10
   least agreement   most agreement
2. 1   2   3   4   5   6   7   8   9   10
   least agreement   most agreement
3. 1   2   3   4   5   6   7   8   9   10
   least agreement   most agreement

4. 1   2   3   4   5   6   7   8   9   10
   least agreement   most agreement
5. 1   2   3   4   5   6   7   8   9   10
   least agreement   most agreement
6. 1   2   3   4   5   6   7   8   9   10
   least agreement   most agreement

7. 1   2   3   4   5   6   7   8   9   10
   least agreement   most agreement
8. 1   2   3   4   5   6   7   8   9   10
   least agreement   most agreement
9. 1   2   3   4   5   6   7   8   9   10
   least agreement   most agreement

10. 1   2   3   4   5   6   7   8   9   10
    least agreement   most agreement
11. 1   2   3   4   5   6   7   8   9   10
    least agreement   most agreement
12. 1   2   3   4   5   6   7   8   9   10
    least agreement   most agreement

13. 1   2   3   4   5   6   7   8   9   10
    least agreement   most agreement
14. 1   2   3   4   5   6   7   8   9   10
    least agreement   most agreement
15. 1   2   3   4   5   6   7   8   9   10
    least agreement   most agreement

16. 1   2   3   4   5   6   7   8   9   10
    least agreement   most agreement
17. 1   2   3   4   5   6   7   8   9   10
    least agreement   most agreement
18. 1   2   3   4   5   6   7   8   9   10
    least agreement   most agreement

Quick Test Score Sheet (cont.)

19. 1   2   3   4   5   6   7   8   9   10
least agreement   most agreement

20. 1   2   3   4   5   6   7   8   9   10
least agreement   most agreement

21. 1   2   3   4   5   6   7   8   9   10
least agreement   most agreement

22. 1   2   3   4   5   6   7   8   9   10
least agreement   most agreement

23. 1   2   3   4   5   6   7   8   9   10
least agreement   most agreement

24. 1   2   3   4   5   6   7   8   9   10
least agreement   most agreement

25. 1   2   3   4   5   6   7   8   9   10
least agreement   most agreement

26. 1   2   3   4   5   6   7   8   9   10
least agreement   most agreement

27. 1   2   3   4   5   6   7   8   9   10
least agreement   most agreement

Transfer your scores from the score sheet to the following boxes. Total the scores in each of the nine boxes.

Quick Test Boxes

1._____	4._____	7._____
2._____	5._____	8._____
3._____	6._____	9._____
Total _____	Total _____	Total _____
Personality Type One	Personality Type Two	Personality Type Three

10._____	13._____	16._____
11._____	14._____	17._____
12._____	15._____	18._____
Total _____	Total _____	Total _____
Personality Type Four	Personality Type Five	Personality Type Six

19._____	22._____	25._____
20._____	23._____	26._____
21._____	24._____	27._____
Total _____	Total _____	Total _____
Personality Type Seven	Personality Type Eight	Personality Type Nine

True or False Score Sheet

Ones	Twos	Threes	Fours	Fives	Sixes	Sevens	Eights	Nines
1.___	1.___	1.___	1.___	1.___	1.___	1.___	1.___	1.___
2.___	2.___	2.___	2.___	2.___	2.___	2.___	2.___	2.___
3.___	3.___	3.___	3.___	3.___	3.___	3.___	3.___	3.___
4.___	4.___	4.___	4.___	4.___	4.___	4.___	4.___	4.___
5.___	5.___	5.___	5.___	5.___	5.___	5.___	5.___	5.___
6.___	6.___	6.___	6.___	6.___	6.___	6.___	6.___	6.___
7.___	7.___	7.___	7.___	7.___	7.___	7.___	7.___	8.___
8.___	8.___	8.___	8.___	8.___	8.___	8.___	8.___	8.___
9.___	9.___	9.___	9.___	9.___	9.___	9.___	9.___	9.___
10.___	10.___	10.___	10.___	10.___	10.___	10.___	10.___	10.___
11.___	11.___	11.___	11.___	11.___	11.___	11.___	11.___	11.___
12.___	12.___	12.___	12.___	12.___	12.___	12.___	12.___	12.___
13.___	13.___	13.___	13.___	13.___	13.___	13.___	13.___	13.___
14.___	14.___	14.___	14.___	14.___	14.___	14.___	14.___	14.___
15.___	15.___	15.___	15.___	15.___	15.___	15.___	15.___	15.___
16.___	16.___	16.___	16.___	16.___	16.___	16.___	16.___	16.___
17.___	17.___	17.___	17.___	17.___	17.___	17.___	17.___	17.___
18.___	18.___	18.___	18.___	18.___	18.___	18.___	18.___	18.___
19.___	19.___	19.___	19.___	19.___	19.___	19.___	19.___	19.___
20.___	20.___	20.___	20.___	20.___	20.___	20.___	20.___	20.___
21.___	21.___	21.___	21.___	21.___	21.___	21.___	21.___	21.___
22.___	22.___	22.___	22.___	22.___	22.___	22.___	22.___	22.___
23.___	23.___	23.___	23.___	23.___	23.___	23.___	23.___	23.___
24.___	24.___	24.___	24.___	24.___	24.___	24.___	24.___	24.___
25.___	25.___	25.___	25.___	25.___	25.___	25.___	25.___	25.___
26.___	26.___	26.___	26.___	26.___	26.___	26.___	26.___	26.___
27.___	27.___	27.___	27.___	27.___	27.___	27.___	27.___	27.___
28.___	28.___	28.___	28.___	28.___	28.___	28.___	28.___	28.___
29.___	29.___	29.___	29.___	29.___	29.___	29.___	29.___	29.___
30.___	30.___	30.___	30.___	30.___	30.___	30.___	30.___	30.___
31.___	31.___	31.___	31.___	31.___	31.___	31.___	31.___	31.___
32.___	32.___	32.___	32.___	32.___	32.___	32.___	32.___	32.___
33.___	33.___	33.___	33.___	33.___	33.___	33.___	33.___	33.___
34.___	34.___	34.___	34.___	34.___	34.___	34.___	34.___	34.___
35.___	35.___	35.___	35.___	35.___	35.___	35.___	35.___	35.___
36.___	36.___	36.___	36.___	36.___	36.___	36.___	36.___	36.___
37.___	37.___	37.___	37.___	37.___	37.___	37.___	37.___	37.___
38.___	38.___	38.___	38.___	38.___	38.___	38.___	38.___	38.___
39.___	39.___	39.___	39.___	39.___	39.___	39.___	39.___	39.___
40.___	40.___	40.___	40.___	40.___	40.___	40.___	40.___	40.___
41.___	41.___	41.___	41.___	41.___	41.___	41.___	41.___	41.___
42.___	42.___	42.___	42.___	42.___	42.___	42.___	42.___	42.___
43.___	43.___	43.___	43.___	43.___	43.___	43.___	43.___	43.___
44.___	44.___	44.___	44.___	44.___	44.___	44.___	44.___	44.___
45.___	45.___	45.___	45.___	45.___	45.___	45.___	45.___	45.___
46.___	46.___	46.___	46.___	46.___	46.___	46.___	46.___	46.___
47.___	47.___	47.___	47.___	47.___	47.___	47.___	47.___	47.___
48.___	48.___	48.___	48.___	48.___	48.___	48.___	48.___	48.___
49.___	49.___	49.___	49.___	49.___	49.___	49.___	49.___	49.___
50.___	50.___	50.___	50.___	50.___	50.___	50.___	50.___	50.___
SCORE	SCORE	SCORE	SCORE	SCORE	SCORE	SCORE	SCORE	SCORE

Quick Test Score Sheet

1. 1   2   3   4   5   6   7   8   9   10

least agreement   most agreement

2. 1   2   3   4   5   6   7   8   9   10

least agreement   most agreement

3. 1   2   3   4   5   6   7   8   9   10

least agreement   most agreement

4. 1   2   3   4   5   6   7   8   9   10

least agreement   most agreement

5. 1   2   3   4   5   6   7   8   9   10

least agreement   most agreement

6. 1   2   3   4   5   6   7   8   9   10

least agreement   most agreement

7. 1   2   3   4   5   6   7   8   9   10

least agreement   most agreement

8. 1   2   3   4   5   6   7   8   9   10

least agreement   most agreement

9. 1   2   3   4   5   6   7   8   9   10

least agreement   most agreement

10. 1   2   3   4   5   6   7   8   9   10

least agreement   most agreement

11. 1   2   3   4   5   6   7   8   9   10

least agreement   most agreement

12. 1   2   3   4   5   6   7   8   9   10

least agreement   most agreement

13. 1   2   3   4   5   6   7   8   9   10

least agreement   most agreement

14. 1   2   3   4   5   6   7   8   9   10

least agreement   most agreement

15. 1   2   3   4   5   6   7   8   9   10

least agreement   most agreement

16. 1   2   3   4   5   6   7   8   9   10

least agreement   most agreement

17. 1   2   3   4   5   6   7   8   9   10

least agreement   most agreement

18. 1   2   3   4   5   6   7   8   9   10

least agreement   most agreement

Quick Test Score Sheet (cont.)

19. 1   2   3   4   5   6   7   8   9   10
    least agreement   most agreement

20. 1   2   3   4   5   6   7   8   9   10
    least agreement   most agreement

21. 1   2   3   4   5   6   7   8   9   10
    least agreement   most agreement

22. 1   2   3   4   5   6   7   8   9   10
    least agreement   most agreement

23. 1   2   3   4   5   6   7   8   9   10
    least agreement   most agreement

24. 1   2   3   4   5   6   7   8   9   10
    least agreement   most agreement

25. 1   2   3   4   5   6   7   8   9   10
    least agreement   most agreement

26. 1   2   3   4   5   6   7   8   9   10
    least agreement   most agreement

27. 1   2   3   4   5   6   7   8   9   10
    least agreement   most agreement

Transfer your scores from the score sheet to the following boxes. Total the scores in each of the nine boxes.

Quick Test Boxes

1._____ 2._____ 3._____ Total _____ Personality Type One	4._____ 5._____ 6._____ Total _____ Personality Type Two	7._____ 8._____ 9._____ Total _____ Personality Type Three
10._____ 11._____ 12._____ Total _____ Personality Type Four	13._____ 14._____ 15._____ Total _____ Personality Type Five	16._____ 17._____ 18._____ Total _____ Personality Type Six
19._____ 20._____ 21._____ Total _____ Personality Type Seven	22._____ 23._____ 24._____ Total _____ Personality Type Eight	25._____ 26._____ 27._____ Total _____ Personality Type Nine

True or False Score Sheet

Ones	Twos	Threes	Fours	Fives	Sixes	Sevens	Eights	Nines
1.	1.	1.	1.	1.	1.	1.	1.	1.
2.	2.	2.	2.	2.	2.	2.	2.	2.
3.	3.	3.	3.	3.	3.	3.	3.	3.
4.	4.	4.	4.	4.	4.	4.	4.	4.
5.	5.	5.	5.	5.	5.	5.	5.	5.
6.	6.	6.	6.	6.	6.	6.	6.	6.
7.	7.	7.	7.	7.	7.	7.	7.	8.
8.	8.	8.	8.	8.	8.	8.	8.	8.
9.	9.	9.	9.	9.	9.	9.	9.	9.
10.	10.	10.	10.	10.	10.	10.	10.	10.
11.	11.	11.	11.	11.	11.	11.	11.	11.
12.	12.	12.	12.	12.	12.	12.	12.	12.
13.	13.	13.	13.	13.	13.	13.	13.	13.
14.	14.	14.	14.	14.	14.	14.	14.	14.
15.	15.	15.	15.	15.	15.	15.	15.	15.
16.	16.	16.	16.	16.	16.	16.	16.	16.
17.	17.	17.	17.	17.	17.	17.	17.	17.
18.	18.	18.	18.	18.	18.	18.	18.	18.
19.	19.	19.	19.	19.	19.	19.	19.	19.
20.	20.	20.	20.	20.	20.	20.	20.	20.
21.	21.	21.	21.	21.	21.	21.	21.	21.
22.	22.	22.	22.	22.	22.	22.	22.	22.
23.	23.	23.	23.	23.	23.	23.	23.	23.
24.	24.	24.	24.	24.	24.	24.	24.	24.
25.	25.	25.	25.	25.	25.	25.	25.	25.
26.	26.	26.	26.	26.	26.	26.	26.	26.
27.	27.	27.	27.	27.	27.	27.	27.	27.
28.	28.	28.	28.	28.	28.	28.	28.	28.
29.	29.	29.	29.	29.	29.	29.	29.	29.
30.	30.	30.	30.	30.	30.	30.	30.	30.
31.	31.	31.	31.	31.	31.	31.	31.	31.
32.	32.	32.	32.	32.	32.	32.	32.	32.
33.	33.	33.	33.	33.	33.	33.	33.	33.
34.	34.	34.	34.	34.	34.	34.	34.	34.
35.	35.	35.	35.	35.	35.	35.	35.	35.
36.	36.	36.	36.	36.	36.	36.	36.	36.
37.	37.	37.	37.	37.	37.	37.	37.	37.
38.	38.	38.	38.	38.	38.	38.	38.	38.
39.	39.	39.	39.	39.	39.	39.	39.	39.
40.	40.	40.	40.	40.	40.	40.	40.	40.
41.	41.	41.	41.	41.	41.	41.	41.	41.
42.	42.	42.	42.	42.	42.	42.	42.	42.
43.	43.	43.	43.	43.	43.	43.	43.	43.
44.	44.	44.	44.	44.	44.	44.	44.	44.
45.	45.	45.	45.	45.	45.	45.	45.	45.
46.	46.	46.	46.	46.	46.	46.	46.	46.
47.	47.	47.	47.	47.	47.	47.	47.	47.
48.	48.	48.	48.	48.	48.	48.	48.	48.
49.	49.	49.	49.	49.	49.	49.	49.	49.
50.	50.	50.	50.	50.	50.	50.	50.	50.
SCORE	SCORE	SCORE	SCORE	SCORE	SCORE	SCORE	SCORE	SCORE

Quick Test Score Sheet

1. 1   2   3   4   5   6   7 .   8   9   10
   least agreement   most agreement
2. 1   2   3   4   5   6   7   8   9   10
   least agreement   most agreement
3. 1   2   3   4   5   6   7   8   9   10
   least agreement   most agreement

4. 1   2   3   4   5   6   7   8   9   10
   least agreement   most agreement
5. 1   2   3   4   5   6   7   8   9   10
   least agreement   most agreement
6. 1   2   3   4   5   6   7   8   9   10
   least agreement   most agreement

7. 1   2   3   4   5   6   7   8   9   10
   least agreement   most agreement
8. 1   2   3   4   5   6   7   8   9   10
   least agreement   most agreement
9. 1   2   3   4   5   6   7   8   9   10
   least agreement   most agreement

10. 1   2   3   4   5   6   7   8   9   10
    least agreement   most agreement
11. 1   2   3   4   5   6   7   8   9   10
    least agreement   most agreement
12. 1   2   3   4   5   6   7   8   9   10
    least agreement   most agreement

13. 1   2   3   4   5   6   7   8   9   10
    least agreement   most agreement
14. 1   2   3   4   5   6   7   8   9   10
    least agreement   most agreement
15. 1   2   3   4   5   6   7   8   9   10
    least agreement   most agreement

16. 1   2   3   4   5   6   7   8   9   10
    least agreement   most agreement
17. 1   2   3   4   5   6   7   8   9   10
    least agreement   most agreement
18. 1   2   3   4   5   6   7   8   9   10
    least agreement   most agreement

Quick Test Score Sheet (cont.)

19.	1	2	3	4	5	6	7	8	9	10
	least agreement							most agreement		
20.	1	2	3	4	5	6	7	8	9	10
	least agreement							most agreement		
21.	1	2	3	4	5	6	7	8	9	10
	least agreement							most agreement		
22.	1	2	3	4	5	6	7	8	9	10
	least agreement							most agreement		
23.	1	2	3	4	5	6	7	8	9	10
	least agreement							most agreement		
24.	1	2	3	4	5	6	7	8	9	10
	least agreement							most agreement		
25.	1	2	3	4	5	6	7	8	9	10
	least agreement							most agreement		
26.	1	2	3	4	5	6	7	8	9	10
	least agreement							most agreement		
27.	1	2	3	4	5	6	7	8	9	10
	least agreement							most agreement		

Transfer your scores from the score sheet to the following boxes. Total the scores in each of the nine boxes.

Quick Test Boxes

1._____
2._____
3._____
Total _____
Personality
Type One

4._____
5._____
6._____
Total _____
Personality
Type Two

7._____
8._____
9._____
Total _____
Personality
Type Three

10._____
11._____
12._____
Total _____
Personality
Type Four

13._____
14._____
15._____
Total _____
Personality
Type Five

16._____
17._____
18._____
Total _____
Personality
Type Six

19._____
20._____
21._____
Total _____
Personality
Type Seven

22._____
23._____
24._____
Total _____
Personality
Type Eight

25._____
26._____
27._____
Total _____
Personality
Type Nine

True or False Score Sheet

Ones	Twos	Threes	Fours	Fives	Sixes	Sevens	Eights	Nines
1.___	1.___	1.___	1.___	1.___	1.___	1.___	1.___	1.___
2.___	2.___	2.___	2.___	2.___	2.___	2.___	2.___	2.___
3.___	3.___	3.___	3.___	3.___	3.___	3.___	3.___	3.___
4.___	4.___	4.___	4.___	4.___	4.___	4.___	4.___	4.___
5.___	5.___	5.___	5.___	5.___	5.___	5.___	5.___	5.___
6.___	6.___	6.___	6.___	6.___	6.___	6.___	6.___	6.___
7.___	7.___	7.___	7.___	7.___	7.___	7.___	7.___	8.___
8.___	8.___	8.___	8.___	8.___	8.___	8.___	8.___	8.___
9.___	9.___	9.___	9.___	9.___	9.___	9.___	9.___	9.___
10.___	10.___	10.___	10.___	10.___	10.___	10.___	10.___	10.___
11.___	11.___	11.___	11.___	11.___	11.___	11.___	11.___	11.___
12.___	12.___	12.___	12.___	12.___	12.___	12.___	12.___	12.___
13.___	13.___	13.___	13.___	13.___	13.___	13.___	13.___	13.___
14.___	14.___	14.___	14.___	14.___	14.___	14.___	14.___	14.___
15.___	15.___	15.___	15.___	15.___	15.___	15.___	15.___	15.___
16.___	16.___	16.___	16.___	16.___	16.___	16.___	16.___	16.___
17.___	17.___	17.___	17.___	17.___	17.___	17.___	17.___	17.___
18.___	18.___	18.___	18.___	18.___	18.___	18.___	18.___	18.___
19.___	19.___	19.___	19.___	19.___	19.___	19.___	19.___	19.___
20.___	20.___	20.___	20.___	20.___	20.___	20.___	20.___	20.___
21.___	21.___	21.___	21.___	21.___	21.___	21.___	21.___	21.___
22.___	22.___	22.___	22.___	22.___	22.___	22.___	22.___	22.___
23.___	23.___	23.___	23.___	23.___	23.___	23.___	23.___	23.___
24.___	24.___	24.___	24.___	24.___	24.___	24.___	24.___	24.___
25.___	25.___	25.___	25.___	25.___	25.___	25.___	25.___	25.___
26.___	26.___	26.___	26.___	26.___	26.___	26.___	26.___	26.___
27.___	27.___	27.___	27.___	27.___	27.___	27.___	27.___	27.___
28.___	28.___	28.___	28.___	28.___	28.___	28.___	28.___	28.___
29.___	29.___	29.___	29.___	29.___	29.___	29.___	29.___	29.___
30.___	30.___	30.___	30.___	30.___	30.___	30.___	30.___	30.___
31.___	31.___	31.___	31.___	31.___	31.___	31.___	31.___	31.___
32.___	32.___	32.___	32.___	32.___	32.___	32.___	32.___	32.___
33.___	33.___	33.___	33.___	33.___	33.___	33.___	33.___	33.___
34.___	34.___	34.___	34.___	34.___	34.___	34.___	34.___	34.___
35.___	35.___	35.___	35.___	35.___	35.___	35.___	35.___	35.___
36.___	36.___	36.___	36.___	36.___	36.___	36.___	36.___	36.___
37.___	37.___	37.___	37.___	37.___	37.___	37.___	37.___	37.___
38.___	38.___	38.___	38.___	38.___	38.___	38.___	38.___	38.___
39.___	39.___	39.___	39.___	39.___	39.___	39.___	39.___	39.___
40.___	40.___	40.___	40.___	40.___	40.___	40.___	40.___	40.___
41.___	41.___	41.___	41.___	41.___	41.___	41.___	41.___	41.___
42.___	42.___	42.___	42.___	42.___	42.___	42.___	42.___	42.___
43.___	43.___	43.___	43.___	43.___	43.___	43.___	43.___	43.___
44.___	44.___	44.___	44.___	44.___	44.___	44.___	44.___	44.___
45.___	45.___	45.___	45.___	45.___	45.___	45.___	45.___	45.___
46.___	46.___	46.___	46.___	46.___	46.___	46.___	46.___	46.___
47.___	47.___	47.___	47.___	47.___	47.___	47.___	47.___	47.___
48.___	48.___	48.___	48.___	48.___	48.___	48.___	48.___	48.___
49.___	49.___	49.___	49.___	49.___	49.___	49.___	49.___	49.___
50.___	50.___	50.___	50.___	50.___	50.___	50.___	50.___	50.___	50.___
SCORE	SCORE	SCORE	SCORE	SCORE	SCORE	SCORE	SCORE	SCORE

ALAN FENSIN earned an MBA in behavior analysis from Tulane University and worked as an electrical engineer on the Apollo space program. He believes that the enneagram changed his life, exposing secrets about his personality that had previously limited his career.

GEORGE RYAN, the coauthor of a number of health and psychology books, is a senior editor of *Longevity* magazine.

BARRY LOPEZ

**DESERT NOTES: Reflections in the Eye of the Raven and
RIVER NOTES: The Dance of Herons**

71110-9/$7.95 US/$9.95 Can

"Barry Lopez is a landscape artist who paints images with sparse,
elegant strokes…His prose is as smooth as river rocks."

Oregon Journal

GIVING BIRTH TO THUNDER,   71111-7
SLEEPING WITH HIS DAUGHTER $7.95 US/$9.95 CAN

In 68 tales from 42 American Indian tribes, Lopez recreates the
timeless adventures and rueful wisdom of Old Man Coyote, an
American Indian hero with a thousand faces—and a thousand
tricks.

Coming Soon

WINTER COUNT   71937-1/$7.00 US/$9.00 Can

Quiet, intoxicating tales of revelation and woe evoke beauty from
darkness, magic without manipulation, and memory without
remorse.